M000100702

Cultural Diversity:

Building Skills for Awareness, Understanding and Application

Third Edition

Barbara Heuberger, Ph.D

Associate Professor
Miami University

KENDALL/HUNT PUBLISHING COMPANY
4050 Westmark Drive   Dubuque, Iowa 52002

Book ordering information:

Telephone: 800–228–0810
Fax: 800–772–9165
Web site: www.kendallhunt.com

Front and back cover photographs by Barbara Heuberger.

Copyright © 2000, 2001, 2004 by Barbara Heuberger

ISBN 978-0-7575-1375-6

Kendall/Hunt Publishing Company has the exclusive rights to
reproduce this work, to prepare derivative works from this work,
to publicly distribute this work, to publicly perform this work and
to publicly display this work.

All rights reserved. No part of this publication may be reproduced,
stored in a retrieval system, or transmitted, in any form or by any
means, electronic, mechanical, photocopying, recording, or otherwise,
without the prior written permission of the copyright owner.

Printed in the United States of America
10 9 8 7 6

Contents

Chapter 3: Why Awareness, Understanding and Application of Diversity Issues Are Important   61

Chapter 4: Cultural Programming, Conflict and Conflict Resolution, and Use of Language   77

PART II: UNDERSTANDING   95

Chapter 7: Case Studies in Exploring Characteristics and Systems of Culture   143

Foreword

As the former Provost and Executive Vice President for Academic Affairs at Miami University, I feel strongly about assisting students to develop a greater awareness and understanding of diversity and multiculturalism as essential preparation for future roles in their professions and as global citizens. This book is a resource in achieving that goal and in meeting our responsibilities in colleges and universities. I am therefore pleased to write this foreword for *Cultural Diversity: Building Skills for Awareness, Understanding and Application*.

At Miami University, this book is used in an introductory diversity course entitled "Strength Through Cultural Diversity." Since the 1996-97 academic year, the course has been taught by faculty from all divisions of the university and has been completed by over 3000 students. The course is a success story of curricular diversity initiatives—the initial development of the course was by a small group of people in the School of Applied Science and over time grew to be an integral part of the education of students from many majors on campus.

The course and the book also strongly integrate the values of liberal education that are central to the mission of Miami University. The Miami Plan for Liberal Education requires all students to take courses that meet four identified principles of liberal education: (a) thinking critically, (b) understanding contexts, (c) engaging with other learners and (d) reflecting and acting. Throughout *Cultural Diversity: Building Skills for Awareness, Understanding and Application*, the four principles of liberal education are both thoughtfully and thoroughly infused into the content, examples, activities and discussion questions. These four principles are at the heart of exploration of cultural diversity. The book provides a strong curricular tool for both the teaching and learning of diversity-related concepts.

Further, the emphasis in the book on both principles of liberal education and student developmental processes provides a model for the exploration of ideas and topics beyond those that are explicitly diversity related. Any content involving the values and beliefs of people where differences exist are implicitly diversity related. Since it can be argued that all academic disciplines have inherent values and assumptions, all disciplines can benefit from exploring those values and assumptions.

Awareness and understanding of cultural diversity is not about political correctness or establishing dichotomous views on issues. It is about how differences between people in their values and beliefs enhance and challenge our understanding of others and ourselves. I appreciate the extensive insight and expertise Dr. Heuberger has skillfully brought to her work in *Cultural Diversity: Building Skills for Awareness, Understanding and Application*. I look forward to the contributions the book will make in assisting those of us who are actively engaged in higher education to fully prepare our students for their futures and ours.

Dr. Ronald Crutcher
President, Wheaton College

Preface

This book was written to assist college students in developing skills in diversity and multiculturalism that can be applied to many contexts. The title *Cultural Diversity: Building Skills for Awareness, Understanding and Application* was selected to emphasize mastering a developmental framework for becoming aware of, understanding, and applying diversity-related concepts to a wide variety of situations.

Diversity is broadly defined in the book and includes many types of difference, such as religion, gender, disability, sexual orientation, class, communication styles and other personal characteristics, race, skin color and ethnicity. Types of diversity are infused throughout the book (rather than segmented into individual chapters) to illustrate multiple diversities. Constructed to be introductory in nature, this book provides a grounding for an initial exploration of diversity concepts.

The process used in the book enables students to become more aware of their own values and beliefs. Thinking about diversity from a personal perspective gives the student ownership of the topic and is the cornerstone of increasing student awareness and understanding of other people and types of diversity. A greater level of awareness is coupled throughout the book with activities and examples to help students understand both differences and similarities between individuals and groups. Applying the skills of increasing awareness and developing understanding is used to analyze issues and events.

The emphasis on student developmental levels and using a process that builds skills is central to the book. The process is not linear. Concepts that are introduced early are reinforced with more challenging examples and activities throughout the book. The activities help students to think more deeply about their own beliefs and values as well as the beliefs and values of others in local, national and global contexts.

Part I (Chapters 1 through 4) focuses on building awareness through discussions of central diversity concepts and self-exploration of values and beliefs about diversity-related issues. These chapters introduce types of diversity and important diversity concepts such as ethnocentrism, stereotyping and dominant privilege. The chapters assist students in identifying the importance of awareness of diversity in their personal and professional lives.

Part II (Chapters 5 through 7) introduces and applies a conceptual framework for increased understanding of culture and diversity. These chapters focus on the characteristics and systems of culture as well as underlying values and beliefs that create and support cultures. Students use their own examples and experiences to help them understand the experiences of others. National and global issues and events are also used to think deeply about culture and types of diversity.

Part III (Chapters 8 and 9) applies diversity concepts in a variety of ways. Chapter 8 uses examples of diversity-related legislation, myths about discrimination and examples of speeches and quotes to illustrate the relationship of perceptions about diversity (e.g., values and beliefs) and laws and policies related to diversity. Chapter 9 guides the students in developing personal diversity plans, including strategies for present and future diversity challenges.

Acknowledgments

This book would not have been written without the initial diversity efforts of David Haddad, former Dean of the School of Applied Sciences at Miami University and current Vice President of Academic Affairs at Loyola College in Baltimore, Maryland. Dr. Haddad's vision was to make Miami University more welcoming to all students and to more effectively prepare students for a multicultural world. Initial work by Dean Haddad, Assistant Dean Christine Noble, Assistant Professor Diane Gerber and others led to the development and implementation of Interdisciplinary Studies (IDS) 159 that led to the development of this book.

There are hundreds of students who have taken the diversity course at Miami and contributed their perspectives to my understanding of students' perceptions of diversity. In addition, many faculty from a variety of academic disciplines have taught the course, enhancing my appreciation of how different people approach diversity awareness, understanding and application. Many other colleagues from around the United States are deeply committed to issues of diversity and have contributed to my views through numerous discussions about teaching and diversity in the academe.

In the preparation of the book, I am grateful to Wendy Beckman, former Visiting Instructor at Miami University, and Alicia Chávez, Dean of Students at the University of Wisconsin, Madison, for their reviews of the first edition of the manuscript. They brought insight and thoughtfulness in both diversity concepts and student developmental levels to the manuscript. I am also thankful to Ms. Beckman for her extensive copy editing of multiple drafts of all editions of the book. Her efforts in "combing through the tangles" are deeply appreciated.

Finally, I would like to thank John and Brenna Heuberger for their support. "Mommy, are you doing homework again?" was often heard (and thought) at our house during the writing process. Although the answer to my now eight-year-old was usually "Yes, Brenna Rose," the writing process and product will, in the long run, help her understanding the importance of the issues addressed in the book.

Barbara Heuberger

PART I

Awareness

Diversity and Important Concepts

"The real voyage of discovery consists not in seeking new landscapes,
but in having new eyes."

Marcel Proust

"This we know: All things are connected like the blood that unites us.
We do not weave the web of life; we are merely a strand in it.
Whatever we do to the web, we do to ourselves."

Chief Seattle

Objectives of Chapter 1

The overall objective of Chapter 1 is to define diversity in the context in which it will
be used in this book, and to discuss specific concepts that are important in exploring awareness, understanding and application of diversity issues. Many of the concepts in Chapter 1
can be defined in multiple ways and will be examined in depth in other chapters. Specific
objectives for Chapter 1 follow.

❖ Examine dimensions of types of diversity (legal, visible and individual or cultural)
❖ Explore the challenges of multiple diversities within individuals and groups
❖ Define stereotypes, biases and discrimination
❖ Define ethnocentrism
❖ Examine dominant privilege
❖ Explore levels of acceptance of diversity
❖ Define culture and multiculturalism
❖ Identify patterns of assimilation and acculturation

Types of Diversity

For the purpose of this book, human diversity can be broadly defined as difference of any kind between people. Both individuals and cultural groups represent diversity. In other words, every person is similar to and different from every other person in some ways.

There are many types of diversity. When we think of diversity, we often think of characteristics such as race, gender, religion, disability and sexual orientation. There are many other types of diversity that affect interpersonal interaction and the understanding of cultures, such as personality type, communication styles and conflict and negotiation styles, among others.

Diversity can vary on many dimensions. First, law applies to some types of diversity. Federal law prohibits discrimination on the basis of race, color, ethnicity, gender, religion, disability and age. State and local laws may extend the law to provide additional protection. Some states have enacted hate crimes legislation to add penalties to crimes based on racial or other hatred. Some cities, including San Francisco, have passed local ordinances to prevent discrimination based on sexual orientation, body weight and other factors.

It should be noted that discrimination itself is not illegal. Law does not apply to many types of diversity, and discrimination is a part of daily life. Only those types of diversity that are included in federal law are covered against discrimination in all parts of the United States, and global discrimination laws vary tremendously. Discrimination on a daily basis ranges from discriminating among applicants for a job to discriminating among students when assigning grades. A key difference between daily discriminating and illegal or inappropriate discriminating is the basis for the discrimination.

Second, some types of diversity are usually (but not always) visible, such as race and gender. Physical characteristics or appearance may also identify ethnicity, religion or certain types of disability. Since many types of diversity are not indicated by visible characteristics, awareness of diversity on those dimensions may be limited, thus impeding cultural understanding in specific instances.

Third, some types of diversity are individual rather than cultural. For example, income, education, communication style, learning style and geographic location all represent types of diversity and can vary from individual to individual. Even in the classroom, students vary in many ways that affect the way they think about things. Individual dimensions of diversity are likely to be affected by societal or cultural aspects.

ACTIVITY 1.1

1. Individually, write down types of diversity that you represent as an individual. Divide the list by the three categories: legal, visible or invisible, individual or cultural.

2. Describe the dimensions of diversity you have that may affect your learning in this course.

3. As a group, identify as many types of diversity as you can that are represented by the people in the classroom. Divide the list by the same three categories (legally protected classes, visible or invisible, individual or cultural).

4. What does the activity help you understand about yourself and other students in the class?

Complexity of Multiple Diversities

Every person represents multiple forms of diversity. That complexity creates a variety of challenges to diversity awareness and understanding. A first challenge is recognizing that characteristics of a group or culture do not necessarily apply to all individuals within that group. There is a risk of overgeneralizing characteristics of a group, particularly when exploring statistical patterns. An example is that a high percentage of the elderly, people with disabilities, people of color and female single parents have household incomes below the poverty line. However, to assume any individual in any of those groups is in a low-income economic bracket is overgeneralizing. Overgeneralizations may lead to assuming that people from particular groups have characteristics or needs they do not in reality have. This can lead to stereotyping and bias when dealing with individuals.

A second challenge inherent in multiple diversities is that complexity may make analysis of a specific situation difficult. For example, conflict between individuals or groups is often based on multiple differences. Perspectives in a discussion about gender, for example, may be discounted by oversimplifications, such as "He is only saying that because he is a man" or "She is only saying that because she is a woman." These oversimplifications may ignore more important types of diversity related to the context of the situation, such as conflict style of the individual.

ACTIVITY 1.2

1. Give an example of a recent interaction you had with another person.

2. What characteristics of each person assisted the interaction?

3. What characteristics of each person impeded the interaction?

4. Describe as many types of diversity as you can that may have affected the interaction.

5. Discuss how the types of diversity affected the interaction.

Relationship of Diversity to Stereotypes, Bias and Discrimination

Stereotypes, bias and discrimination are concepts that are related to diversity and to each other. Each of the three concepts is related to diversity because each relates to differences between people. The concepts are related to each other because stereotypes can be the basis for bias and bias can be the basis for discrimination.

A stereotype is an attitude or perception about an individual or group based on generalized beliefs about the group. The beliefs may or may not be accurate for the group as a whole, and are unlikely to be accurate for all individuals within the group. For example, there are geographic stereotypes based on states (e.g., Texas, California), cities (e.g., New York, Chicago), regions (e.g., the Southern states) and countries (e.g., Iran, Japan).

Creating stereotypes is a predictable human response to processing the massive amounts of information we are exposed to every day. Everyone generalizes about others. Identifying one's stereotypes and generalizations is a first step to understanding the basis and effects of stereotypes.

Bias refers to a preference toward or against individuals or groups based on an individual or cultural characteristic, or a perceived stereotype. A bias toward one's own child is an example of a (usually) positive bias based on characteristics of families. On the other hand, a basis for bias (and subsequent discrimination) can be a stereotype about a diversity characteristic. For example, negativity against a Southern accent is an example of bias that is based on negative stereotypes about people from Southern states.

Discrimination is acting on a bias by treating a person (or group) differently because of the bias. Using the dialect example, not hiring a person for a job because of the presence of a Southern accent is discriminatory, since the act is based on a bias created from a stereotype, and not on the actual abilities of the individual. The discrimination would probably not be illegal, however, since there are no laws against geographical discrimination.

Although negative stereotypes are more common, positive stereotypes also exist. Both negative and positive stereotypes can result in bias and discrimination that are unfair. An unfair advantage created by a positive stereotype that benefits an individual is usually not considered problematic by the individual, but is often problematic for people who do not benefit from the positive stereotype. Continuing our example of dialects, some Southern accents might be viewed as soft-spoken and genteel, while others are considered to be harsh or uneducated. Someone with a Brahmin Boston accent might be treated differently from someone with a North Boston accent, or might be generalized as more educated than the other, for instance.

ACTIVITY 1.3

1. Give an example of a positive stereotype. What characteristic(s) is/are the source of bias? In what ways might the bias create discrimination?

2. Give an example of a negative stereotype. What characteristic(s) is/are the source of bias? In what ways might the bias create discrimination?

3. Give an example of a situation where a stereotype could lead to bias and discrimination.

Stereotyping

Stereotyping creates a barrier to diversity understanding through erroneous positive or negative perceptions about groups of people and the individuals within those groups. There are a number of characteristics of stereotypes and the process of stereotyping.

♦ Stereotyping is an inevitable result of being human and categorizing information.

♦ Stereotypes can be formed through a first exposure to unfamiliar groups, can be passed down to children in families, can be acquired through friends or can be expressed through the media.

♦ When a stereotype is formed, information that is consistent with the stereotype is remembered and information that is inconsistent with the stereotype is ignored or discounted as an exception.

◆ Once a stereotype is formed, considerable contrary information is required to change the stereotype.

◆ Recognizing one's own stereotypes is a first step to understanding the effects of stereotyping.

Stereotypes exist for all types of diversity, including groups of people, cultures, occupations and geographic regions, among others. Activity 1.4 will help you examine the stereotypes of your college, as well as the origins and accuracy of those stereotypes.

ACTIVITY 1.4

1. List as many stereotypes as you can about students at your campus.

2. Where did the stereotypes you listed originate?

3. How well does the stereotype profile of students at your campus apply to you?

The following activity will help you identify what your stereotypes are and where those stereotypes originated. For each group of people on the list, include at least one positive and one negative stereotype, as well as an exception—someone you know or whom you have heard of who is a member of the group but does not fit the stereotype.

ACTIVITY 1.5

	Positive Stereotype	Negative Stereotype	Exception
People with Southern accents are			
People who are poor are			
African Americans are			
Men are			
Young people are			
European Americans are			
Honors students are			
Latinos/Latinas are			
Appalachians are			
Germans are			
Student athletes are			
Chinese are			
Chinese Americans are			
Sorority women are			
Japanese are			

ACTIVITY 1.5, CONTINUED

	Positive Stereotype	Negative Stereotype	Exception
Japanese Americans are			
Elderly people are			
People who use wheelchairs are			
Jewish people are			
Muslim people are			
Fraternity men are			
Christian people are			
Gay men are			
People who are rich are			
Asian Americans are			
Lesbians are			
Women are			

DISCUSSION QUESTIONS:

1. How can negative stereotypes limit individuals within the stereotyped group?

2. How can positive stereotypes unfairly benefit people within the stereotyped group?

Stereotypes are often at the heart of conflict and other national and global issues. In Activity 1.6, identify national and global issues or current events that are related to stereotyping for the following groups of people. (For example, in race, racial profiling and differential treatment in the criminal justice system would be examples of national issues.)

ACTIVITY 1.6

	National Issue	Global Issue
Age		
Disability status		
Socio-economic status		
Geographic diversity		

ACTIVITY 1.6, CONTINUED

	National Issue	Global Issue
Ethnicity		
Race		
Gender		
Sexual orientation		
Religion		

Relationship of Diversity to Ethnocentrism

Ethnocentrism is the attitude or impression that one's own belief system and culture are superior to the belief systems and cultures of others. Ethnocentrism is often the result of a lack of awareness and understanding beyond one's own experiences. Cultures are the result of a variety of belief systems. Other cultures are often viewed through and judged by one's own ethnocentrism. Ethnocentrism is not necessarily a conscious thought or act.

Examples of ethnocentrism are numerous, and range from individual behaviors to national and international issues and policies. Examples of ethnocentrism include beliefs that holding eating utensils one way is better than another, one learning style is better than another, one religion is better than another, one way of communicating is better than another, the United States is superior to other countries or New York is superior to Chicago.

Ethnocentrism can lead to misunderstanding and conflict. Sometimes it is just having such strong cultural lenses that we do not realize we are misinterpreting what we see or feel. An example is when one friend sells an item to another friend. The friend who receives the money carefully counts it out. The other friend is insulted, thinking the friend counting the money does not trust that the money is all there. In truth, the person counting the money always carefully counts change when money is spent.

Ethnocentrism can also lead to people being left out when the prevailing beliefs are represented. For example, hospitals often provide small packages of toiletries to patients. Many include fine-toothed combs. Most people with curly hair cannot use them. It is not a conscious exclusion; rather, it reflects the assumption that all people have fine, straight hair.

ACTIVITY 1.7

1. During the last 24 hours, what are some examples of interactions you have experienced or observed that could have been affected by ethnocentrism? Define how ethnocentrism affected the interactions.

2. Give an example of an ethnocentrism that you hold. How might your ethnocentric view lead to misunderstanding or unfair treatment of others?

3. Give five examples of ethnocentrism.

4. Describe five words we use to define appropriate behavior (e.g., respect, politeness). For each, describe ways that the words are based on values.

5. Give five examples of national or global issues that are affected by ethnocentrism. Describe how ethnocentrism influences the issues.

Ethnocentrism

Ethnocentrism prevents awareness and understanding of difference by assuming one's own beliefs and behaviors are superior to those of others. There are a number of characteristics of ethnocentrism.

- Feelings of superiority are often not conscious; they are the result of repeated or familiar behaviors.
- Ethnocentrism is often based on lack of personal exposure to differences.
- Ethnocentrism is often the result of a lack of understanding of the reasons for behaviors and how different underlying reasons can lead to different behaviors.

ACTIVITY 1.8

1. Using a blank sheet of paper, draw a map of the town that is the site of your university. Be as detailed as possible.

2. On the back of your map, write about how accurately you think your map shows your college town. What parts do you think are accurate? What parts do you think are inaccurate?

3. Exchange maps with another student. From the other student's map, tell the class three things you know about the student from his or her map (e.g., who lives off campus).

4. How did the maps give you the information about the student?

5. In what ways do the maps illustrate ethnocentric behavior?

6. How might maps be different if drawn by others in the community?

Note: See instructor's guide.

Example: Ethnocentric Perception

During an extended stay in Malta, I was at a meeting with a Maltese government official. We were meeting in a café in the capital city of Valletta, a centuries-old walled city with an impressive city gate entrance and large courtyard just inside the gate.

During our meeting, we began to hear shouting outside. As the shouting became louder, people in the café began to speak in Maltese. The café owner went to the front entrance and closed and locked the large metal doors. The person I was meeting with explained that the people outside were marching to protest the verdict in a murder trial. I was told that the case had political overtones, and that murder in Malta was extremely rare, so the case was a source of national interest and controversy. There had been another protest the day before and several businesses were damaged, so we would be locked in at the café until the police ended the protest.

As the shouting died down, the owner reopened the front door. The government official suggested I leave Valletta for the day. As I reached the courtyard at the city gate, there were many police, mobilized from all over the island to respond to the protest. Although I had spent considerable time in Malta, I had never seen anything like the response to the protest. I took out my camera and snapped a few photographs of a few police, on horseback and wearing riot gear.

A woman approached me and said urgently "You can't take photographs here." "What do you mean?" I responded. "You can't take pictures of police—you will be arrested," she said. I asked her where she was from. Her response was "I am from Germany. I am here on holiday for a week." I later found out that taking photographs of police in Malta is not prohibited.

ACTIVITY 1.9

Use the preceding example to respond to the following.

1. What parts of the example were different from your experiences?

2. What assumptions did the German tourist make?

3. What assumptions were made by the author?

4. How could differences in values and beliefs expressed in this example cause misunderstanding or conflict?

ACTIVITY 1.10

1. Read the article "Body Ritual Among the Nacirema" by Horace Miner.

2. What characteristics of the Nacirema culture are different from those of your culture?

3. What characteristics of the Nacirema culture are similar to those of your culture?

4. Select an activity described in the article. Speculate about why the rituals about that activity exist.

(Note to instructor: See Instructor's Guide.)

Body Ritual Among the Nacirema

Horace M. Miner

The anthropologist has become so familiar with the diversity of ways in which different peoples behave in similar situations that he is not apt to be surprised by even the most exotic customs. In fact, if all of the logically possible combinations of behavior have not been found somewhere in the world, he is apt to suspect that they must be present in some yet undescribed tribe. The point has, in fact, been expressed with respect to clan organization by Murdock (1949:71). In this light, the magical beliefs and practices of the Nacirema present such unusual aspects that it seems desirable to describe them as an example of the extremes to which human behavior can go.

Professor Linton first brought the ritual of the Nacirema to the attention of anthropologists twenty years ago (1936:326), but the culture of this people is still very poorly understood. They are a North American group living in the territory between the Canadian Cree, the Yaqui and Tarahumare of Mexico, and the Carib and Arawak of the Antilles. Little is known of their origin, although tradition states that they came from the east. According to Nacirema mythology, their nation was originated by a culture hero, Notgnihsaw, who is otherwise known for two great feats of strength—the throwing of a piece of wampum across the river Pa-To-Mac and the chopping down of a cherry tree in which the Spirit of Truth resided.

Nacirema culture is characterized by a highly developed market economy which has evolved in a rich natural habitat. While much of the people's time is devoted to economic pursuits, a large part of the fruits of these labors and a considerable portion of the day are spent in ritual activity. The focus of this activity is the human body, the appearance and health of which loom as a dominant concern in the ethos of the people. While such a concern is certainly not unusual, its ceremonial aspects and associated philosophy are unique.

The fundamental belief underlying the whole system appears to be that the human body is ugly and that its natural tendency is to debility and disease. Incarcerated in such a body, man's only hope is to avert these characteristics through the use of the powerful influences of ritual and ceremony. Every household has one or more shrines devoted to this purpose. The more powerful individuals in the society have several shrines in their houses and, in fact, the opulence of a house is often referred to in terms of the number of such ritual centers it possesses. Most houses are of wattle and daub construction, but the shrine rooms of the more wealthy are walled with stone. Poorer families imitate the rich by applying pottery plaques to their shrine walls.

While each family has at least one such shrine, the rituals associated with it are not family ceremonies but are private and secret. The rites are normally only discussed with children, and then only during the period when they are being initiated into these mysteries. I was able, however, to establish sufficient rapport with the natives to examine these shrines and to have the rituals described to me.

The focal point of the shrine is a box or chest which is built into the wall. In this chest are kept the many charms and magical potions without which no native believes he could live. These preparations are secured from a variety of specialized practitioners. The most powerful of these are the medicine men, whose assistance must be rewarded with substantial gifts. However, the medicine men do not provide the curative potions for their clients, but decide what the ingredients should be and then write them down in an ancient and secret language. This writing is understood only by the medicine men and by the herbalists who, for another gift, provide the required charm.

The charm is not disposed of after it has served its purpose, but is placed in the charm-box of the household shrine. As these magical materials are specific for certain ills, and the real or imagined maladies of the people are many, the charm-box is usually full to overflowing. The magical packets are so numerous that people forget what their purposes were and fear to use them again. While the natives are very vague on this point, we can only assume that the idea in retaining all the old magical materials is that their presence in the charm-box, before which the body rituals are conducted, will in some way protect the worshipper.

Beneath the charm-box is a small font. Each day every member of the family, in succession, enters the shrine room, bows his head before the charm-box, mingles different sorts of holy water in the font, and proceeds with a brief rite of ablution. The holy waters are secured from the Water Temple of the community, where the priests conduct elaborate ceremonies to make the liquid ritually pure.

In the hierarchy of magical practitioners, and below the medicine men in prestige, are specialists whose designation is best translated "holy-mouth-men." The Nacirema have an almost pathological horror of and fascination with the mouth, the condition of which is believed to have a supernatural influence on all social relationships. Were it not for the rituals of the mouth, they believe that their teeth would fall out, their gums bleed, their jaws shrink, their friends desert them, and their lovers reject them. They also believe that a strong relationship exists between oral and moral characteristics. For example, there is a ritual ablution of the mouth for children which is supposed to improve their moral fiber.

The daily body ritual performed by everyone includes a mouth-rite. Despite the fact that these people are so punctilious about care of the mouth, this rite involves a practice which strikes the uninitiated stranger as revolting. It was reported to me that the ritual consists of inserting a small bundle of hog hairs into the mouth, along with certain magical powders, and then moving the bundle in a highly formalized series of gestures.

In addition to the private mouth-rite, the people seek out a holy-mouth-man once or twice a year. These practitioners have an impressive set of paraphernalia, consisting of a variety of augers, awls, probes, and prods. The use of these objects in the exorcism of the evils of the mouth involves almost unbelievable ritual torture of the client. The holy-mouth-man opens the client's mouth and, using the above mentioned tools, enlarges any holes which decay may have created in the teeth. Magical materials are put into these holes. If there are no naturally occurring holes in the teeth, large sections of one or more teeth are gouged out so that the supernatural substance can be applied.

In the client's view, the purpose of these ministrations is to arrest decay and to draw friends. The extremely sacred and traditional character of the rite is evident in the fact that the natives return to the holy-mouth-men year after year, despite the fact that their teeth continue to decay.

It is to be hoped that, when a thorough study of the Nacirema is made, there will be careful inquiry into the personality structure of these people. One has but to watch the gleam in the eye of a holy-mouth-man, as he jabs an awl into an exposed nerve, to suspect that a certain amount of sadism is involved. If this can be established, a very interesting pattern emerges, for most of the population shows definite masochistic tendencies. It was to these that Professor Linton referred in discussing a distinctive part of the daily body ritual which is performed only by men. This part of the rite involves scraping and lacerating the surface of the face with a sharp instrument. Special women's rites are performed only four times during each lunar month, but what they lack in frequency is made up in barbarity. As part of this ceremony, women bake their heads in small ovens for about an hour. The theoretically interesting point is that what seems to be a preponderantly masochistic people have developed sadistic specialists.

The medicine men have an imposing temple, or *latipso*, in every community of any size. The more elaborate ceremonies required to treat very sick patients can only be performed at this temple. These ceremonies involve not only the thaumaturge but a permanent group of vestal maidens who move sedately about the temple chambers in distinctive costume and headdress.

The *latipso* ceremonies are so harsh that it is phenomenal that a fair proportion of the really sick natives who enter the temple ever recover. Small children whose indoctrination is still incomplete have been known to resist attempts to take them to the temple because "that is where you go to die." Despite this fact, sick adults are not only willing but eager to undergo the protracted ritual purification, if they can afford to do so. No matter how ill the supplicant or how grave the emergency, the guardians of many temples will not admit a client if he cannot give a rich gift to the custodian. Even after one has gained admission and survived the ceremonies, the guardians will not permit the neophyte to leave until he makes still another gift.

The supplicant entering the temple is first stripped of all his or her clothes. In everyday life the Nacirema avoids exposure of his body and its natural functions. Bathing and excretory acts are performed only in the secrecy of the household shrine, where they are ritualized as part of the body-rites. Psychological shock results from the fact that body secrecy is suddenly lost upon entry into the *latipso*. A man, whose own wife has never seen him in an excretory act, suddenly finds himself naked and assisted by a vestal maiden while he performs his natural functions into a sacred vessel. This sort of ceremonial treatment is necessitated by the fact that the excreta are used by a diviner to ascertain the course and nature of the client's sickness. Female clients, on the other hand, find their naked bodies are subjected to the scrutiny, manipulation, and prodding of the medicine men.

Few supplicants in the temple are well enough to do anything but lie on their hard beds. The daily ceremonies, like the rites of the holy-mouth-men, involve discomfort and torture. With ritual precision the vestals awaken their miserable charges each dawn and roll them about on their beds of pain while performing ablutions, in the formal movements of which the maidens are highly trained. At other times they insert magic wands in the supplicant's mouth or force him to eat substances which are supposed to be healing. From time to time the medicine men come to their clients and jab magically treated needles into their flesh. The fact that these temple ceremonies may not cure, and may even kill the neophyte, in no way decreases the people's faith in the medicine men.

There remains one other kind of practitioner, known as a "listener." This witch-doctor has the power to exorcise the devils that lodge in the heads of people who have been bewitched. The Nacirema believe that parents bewitch their own children. Mothers are particularly suspected of putting a curse on children while teaching them the secret body rituals. The counter-magic of the witch-doctor is unusual in its lack of ritual. The patient simply tells the "listener" all his troubles and fears, beginning with the earliest difficulties he can remember. The memory displayed by the Nacirema in these exorcism sessions is truly remarkable. It is not uncommon for the patient to bemoan the rejection he felt upon being weaned as a babe, and a few individuals even see their troubles going back to the traumatic effects of their own birth.

In conclusion, mention must be made of certain practices which have their base in native aesthetics but which depend upon the pervasive aversion to the natural body and its functions. There are ritual fasts to make fat people thin and ceremonial feasts to make thin people fat. Still other rites are used to make women's breasts larger if they are small and smaller if they are large. General dissatisfaction with breast shape is symbolized in the fact that the ideal form is virtually outside the range of human variation. A few women afflicted with almost inhuman hyper-mammary development are so idolized that they make a handsome living by simply going from village to village and permitting the natives to stare at them for a fee.

Reference has already been made to the fact that excretory functions are ritualized, routinized, and relegated to secrecy. Natural reproductive functions are similarly distorted. Intercourse is taboo as a topic and scheduled as an act. Efforts are made to avoid pregnancy by the use of magical materials or by limiting intercourse to certain phases of the moon. Conception is actually very infrequent. When pregnant, women dress so as to hide their condition. Parturition takes place in secret, without friends or relatives to assist, and the majority of women do not nurse their infants.

Our review of the ritual life of the Nacirema has certainly shown them to be a magic-ridden people. It is hard to understand how they have managed to exist so long under the burdens which they have imposed upon themselves. But even such exotic customs as these take on real meaning when they are viewed with the insight provided by Malinowski when he wrote (1948:70):

> *Looking from far and above, from our high places of safety in the developed civilization, it is easy to see all the crudity and irrelevance of magic. But without its power and guidance early man could not have mastered his practical difficulties as he has done, nor could man have advanced to the higher stages of civilization.*

REFERENCES CITED

Ralph Linton, *The Study of Man*, D. Appleton-Century Co., New York, 1936.
Bronislaw Malinowski, *Magic, Science, and Religion*, The Free Press, Glencoe, 1948.
George P. Murdock, *Social Structure*, The Macmillan Co., New York, 1949.

ACTIVITY 1.11

1. After debriefing about the article "Body Ritual Among the Nacirema," your instructor will divide the class into small groups of three or four people.

2. As a group, write several paragraphs describing a ritual of the university culture, using the writing style of the Miner article (e.g., from an outsider point of view).

3. As a group, read their parts of the story aloud.

Dominant Privilege

Dominant privilege is the advantage that is provided to some groups of people over others without conscious earning of this advantage. Dominant privilege applies to most types of diversity. "Dominant" is not synonymous with "majority." As a group, males have dominant privilege in the United States, for example, even though they are in nearly equal numbers to females.

In the United States, Whites, European-Americans, males, people without disabilities, Christians and heterosexuals are groups that often have dominant privilege. However, privilege is contextual. For example, since people represent multiple diversities, it is not uncommon to be in the dominant group on one characteristic and the nondominant group in another. So the privilege of being male may be outweighed by the fact that a man is gay. Or a hearing person trying to participate in a conversation using American Sign Language will be in the minority in that situation by not knowing the language.

Dominant privilege is a unique concept. It cannot be taught to someone in the same way that some other concepts (e.g., stereotypes) can be taught. Most people recognize that stereotypes exist and can easily identify some. Identifying areas of privilege for those who have it is much more difficult, because it is unconscious (like ethnocentrism), and requires more effort on the part of the learner.

Also, dominant privilege is very personal and hard to accept for some people in the dominant group. To say that someone has an unearned advantage can produce anger ("I have worked for and deserve what I have") or guilt (when there is a recognition that nondominance disadvantages other people).

It is not possible to understand racism, sexism, ageism, ableism, homophobia and other types of discrimination without understanding dominant privilege. Dominant privilege is the umbrella concept that allows for oppression, inequality and other treatment of nondominant groups.

The challenges inherent in exploring dominant relate to the learning framework of this book. As stated earlier, awareness of difference is a prerequisite for understanding difference. The following are assumptions in exploring dominant privilege.

- If you are in the dominant group, you can choose to be aware of difference or choose to not be aware of difference. *That choice is part of your privilege.*
- If you are in the dominant group, you can choose to understand difference or choose to not understand difference. *That choice is part of your privilege.*
- If you are in the dominant group and you choose to be aware of and understand difference, *then you must understand how your privilege is a barrier to doing so.*
- If you are in the dominant group and you choose to be aware of and understand difference, *then you must take responsibility for your own learning. A person in the nondominant group may choose to be a resource, but is not responsible for educating you or justifying his or her perspective.*
- If you are in the dominant group, your motivations for awareness and understanding may be different from those in the nondominant group. *You will want to examine your personal motivations to determine how your privilege affects you.*
- If you are in the dominant group, developing an awareness of your privilege requires *consistent and conscious effort, may be uncomfortable at times, and will be an ongoing and challenging effort.*

White Privilege: Unpacking the Invisible Knapsack

I was taught to see racism only in individual acts of meanness, not in invisible systems conferring dominance on my group

Peggy McIntosh

Through work to bring materials from women's studies into the rest of the curriculum, I have often noticed men's unwillingness to grant that they are overprivileged, even though they may grant that women are disadvantaged. They may say they will work to improve women's status, in the society, the university, or the curriculum, but they can't or won't support the idea of lessening men's. Denials that amount to taboos surround the subject of advantages that men gain from women's disadvantages. These denials protect male privilege from being fully acknowledged, lessened, or ended.

Thinking through unacknowledged male privilege as a phenomenon, I realized that, since hierarchies in our society are interlocking, there was most likely a phenomenon of white privilege that was similarly denied and protected. As a white person, I realized I had been taught about racism as something that puts others at a disadvantage, but had been taught not to see one of its corollary aspects, white privilege, which puts me at an advantage.

I think whites are carefully taught not to recognize white privilege, as males are taught not to recognize male privilege. So I have begun in an untutored way to ask what it is like to have white privilege. I have come to see white privilege as an invisible package of unearned assets that I can count on cashing in each day, but about which I was "meant" to remain oblivious. White privilege is like an invisible weightless knapsack of special provisions, maps, passports, codebooks, visas, clothes, tools, and blank checks.

Describing white privilege makes one newly accountable. As we in Women's Studies work to reveal male privilege and ask men to give up some of their power, so one who writes about having white privilege must ask, "Having described it, what will I do to lessen or end it?"

After I realized the extent to which men work from a base of unacknowledged privilege, I understood that much of their oppressiveness was unconscious. Then I remembered the frequent charges from women of color that white women whom they encounter are oppressive. I began to understand why we are justly seen as oppressive, even when we don't see ourselves that way. I began to count the ways in which I enjoy unearned skin privilege and have been conditioned into oblivion about its existence.

My schooling gave me no training in seeing myself as an oppressor, as an unfairly advantaged person, or as a participant in a damaged culture. I was taught to see myself as an individual whose moral state depended on her individual moral will. My schooling followed the pattern my colleague Elizabeth Minnich has pointed out: whites are taught to think of their lives as morally neutral, normative, and average, and also ideal, so that when we work to benefit others, this is seen as work which will allow "them" to be more like "us."

I decided to try to work on myself at least by identifying some of the daily effects of white privilege in my life. I have chosen those conditions which I think in my case attach somewhat more to skin color privilege than to class, religion, ethnic status, or geographical location, though of course all these other factors are intricately intertwined. As far as I can see, my African American coworkers, friends and acquaintances with whom I come into daily or frequent contact in this particular time, place, and line of work cannot count on most of these conditions.

Copyright © 1988 by Peggy McIntosh. Reprinted by permission. Reprint permissions must be obtained from the author—(781)283-2520.

I usually think of privilege as being a favored state, whether earned or conferred by birth or luck. Yet some of the conditions I have described here work to systematically overempower certain groups. Such privilege simply confers dominance because of one's race or sex.

1. I can if I wish arrange to be in the company of people of my race most of the time.
2. If I should need to move, I can be pretty sure renting or purchasing housing in an area which I can afford and in which I would want to live.
3. I can be pretty sure that my neighbors in such a location will be neutral or pleasant to me.
4. I can go shopping alone most of the time, pretty well assured that I will not be followed or harassed.
5. I can turn on the television or open to the front page of the paper and see people of my race widely represented.
6. When I am told about our national heritage or about "civilization," I am shown that people of my color made it what it is.
7. I can be sure that my children will be given curricular materials that testify to the existence of their race.
8. If I want to, I can be pretty sure of finding a publisher for this piece on white privilege.
9. I can go into a music shop and count on finding the music of my race represented, into a supermarket and find the staple foods which fit with my cultural traditions, into a hairdresser's shop and find someone who can cut my hair.
10. Whether I use checks, credit cards, or cash, I can count on my skin color not to work against the appearance of financial reliability.
11. I can arrange to protect my children most of the time from people who might not like them.
12. I can swear, or dress in second hand clothes, or not answer letters, without having people attribute these choices to the bad morals, the poverty, or the illiteracy of my race.
13. I can speak in public to a powerful male group without putting my race on trial.
14. I can do well in a challenging situation without being called a credit to my race.
15. I am never asked to speak for all the people of my racial group.
16. I can remain oblivious of the language and customs of persons of color who constitute the world's majority without feeling in my culture any penalty for such oblivion.
17. I can criticize our government and talk about how much I fear its policies and behavior without being seen as a cultural outsider.
18. I can be pretty sure that if I ask to talk to "the person in charge," I will be facing a person of my race.
19. If a traffic cop pulls me over or if the IRS audits my tax return, I can be sure I haven't been singled out because of my race.
20. I can easily buy posters, postcards, picture books, greeting cards, dolls, toys, and children's magazines featuring people of my race.
21. I can go home from most meetings of organizations I belong to feeling somewhat tied in, rather than isolated, out-of-place, out numbered, unheard, held at a distance, or feared.
22. I can take a job with an affirmative action employer without having coworkers on the job suspect that I got it because of race.
23. I can choose public accommodation without fearing that people of my race cannot get in or will be mistreated in the places I have chosen.

24. I can be sure that if I need legal or medical help, my race will not work against me.
25. If my day, week, or year is going badly, I need not ask of each negative episode or situation whether it has racial overtones.
26. I can choose blemish cover or bandages in flesh color and have them more or less match my skin.

I repeatedly forgot each of the realizations on this list until I wrote it down. For me white privilege has turned out to be an elusive and fugitive subject. The pressure to avoid it is great, for in facing it I must give up the myth of meritocracy. If these things are true, this is not such a free country; one's life is not what one makes it; many doors open for certain people through no virtues of their own.

In unpacking this invisible knapsack of white privilege, I have listed conditions of daily experience which I once took for granted. Nor did I think of any of these prerequisites as bad for the holder. I now think that we need a more finely differentiated taxonomy of privilege, for some of these varieties are only what one would want for everyone in a just society, and others give license to be ignorant.

I see a pattern running through the matrix of white privilege, a pattern of assumptions which were passed on to me as a white person. There was one main piece of cultural turf; it was my own turf, and I was among those who could control the turf. My skin color was an asset for any move I was educated to want to make. I could think of myself as belonging in major ways, and of making social systems work for me. I could freely disparage, fear, neglect, or be oblivious to anything outside of the dominant cultural forms. Being of the main culture, I could also criticize it fairly freely.

In proportion as my racial group was being made confident, comfortable, and oblivious, other groups were likely being made unconfident, uncomfortable, and alienated. Whiteness protected me from many kinds of hostility, distress, and violence, which I was being subtly trained to visit in turn upon people of color. For this reason, the word "privilege" now seems to me misleading. We want, then, to distinguish between earned strength and unearned power conferred systematically. Power from unearned privilege can look like strength when it is in fact permission to escape or to dominate. But not all of the privileges on my list are inevitably damaging. Some, like the expectation that neighbors will be decent to you, or that your race will not count against you in court, should be the norm in a just society. Others, like the privilege to ignore less powerful people, distort the humanity of the holders as well as the ignored groups.

We might at least start by distinguishing between positive advantages which we can work to spread, and negative types of advantages which unless rejected will always reinforce our present hierarchies. For example, the feeling that one belongs within the human circle, as Native Americans say, should not be seen as privilege for a few. Ideally it is an unearned entitlement. At present, since only a few have it, it is an unearned advantage for them. This paper results from a process of coming to see that some of the power which I originally saw as attendant on being a human being in the U.S. consisted in unearned advantage and conferred dominance.

I have met very few men who are truly distressed about systemic, unearned male advantage and conferred dominance. And so one question for me and others like me is whether we will be like them, or whether we will get truly distressed, even outraged, about unearned race advantage and conferred dominance and if so, what we will do to lessen them. In any case, we need to do more work in identifying how they actually affect our daily lives. Many, perhaps most, of our white students in the U.S. think that racism doesn't affect them because they are not people of color; they do not see "whiteness" as a racial identity. In addition, since race and sex are not the only advantaging systems at work, we need similarly to examine the daily experience of having age advantage, or ethnic advantage, or physical ability, or advantage related to nationality, religion, or sexual orientation.

Difficulties and dangers surrounding the task of finding parallels are many. Since racism, sexism, and heterosexism are not the same, the advantaging associated with them should not be seen as the same. In addition, it is hard to disentangle aspects of unearned advantage which rest more on social class, economic class, race, religion, sex and ethnic identity than on other factors. Still, all of the oppressions are interlocking, as the Combahee River Collective Statement of 1977 continues to remind us eloquently. One factor seems clear about all of the interlocking oppressions. They take both active forms which we can see and embedded forms which as a member of the dominant group one is taught not to see. In my class and place, I did not see myself as a racist because I was taught to recognize racism only in individual acts of meanness by members of my group, never in invisible systems conferring unsought racial dominance on my group from birth.

Disapproving of the systems won't be enough to change them. I was taught to think that racism could end if white individuals changed their attitudes. But a white skin in the United States opens many doors for whites whether or not we approve of the way dominance has been conferred on us. Individual acts can palliate, but cannot end, these problems.

To redesign social systems we need first to acknowledge their colossal unseen dimensions. The silences and denials surrounding privilege are the key political tool here. They keep the thinking about equality or equity incomplete, protecting unearned advantage and conferred dominance by making these taboo subjects. Most talk by whites about equal opportunity seems to be now to be about equal opportunity to try to get into a position of dominance while denying that systems of dominance exist.

It seems to me that obliviousness about white advantage, like obliviousness about male advantage, is kept strongly inculturated in the United States so as to maintain the myth of meritocracy, the myth that democratic choice is equally available to all. Keeping most people unaware that freedom of confident action is there for just a small number of people props up those in power, and serves to keep power in the hands of the same groups that have most of it already.

Though systemic change takes many decades, there are pressing questions for me and I imagine for some others like me if we raise our daily consciousness on the perquisites of being light skinned. What will we do with such knowledge? As we know from watching men, it is an open question whether we will choose to use unearned advantage to weaken hidden systems of advantage, and whether we will use any of our arbitrarily awarded power to try to reconstruct power systems on a broader base.

ACTIVITY 1.12

1. Respond to McIntosh's numbered list of 26 privileges, indicating those which you feel you have as privileges.

2. For those privileges that you have, what is the impact of having privilege on you? What is the impact on not having the privilege for those who don't?

3. In pairs or small groups, create additions to the McIntosh list of privilege examples.

ACTIVITY 1.13

Respond to the following quote from Peggy McIntosh.

I was taught to see racism only in individual acts of meanness, not in invisible systems conferring dominance on my group.

1. How was your awareness of privilege different from or similar to the quote before reading her essay?

2. Do you agree or disagree that racism includes privilege? Discuss your answer.

3. In what ways can you work to increase your awareness of your own privileges?

Activity 1.14

Complete the table, answering each of the following three questions.

1. In what characteristics are you a member of the dominant (or more powerful) culture of the United States? (check all that apply)

2. For all "yes" answers, list an advantage that you have by being in the dominant group.

3. For all "no" answers, list a way that being in the nondominant group disadvantages you.

	If yes, list an advantage you have	If no, list a way that you are disadvantaged
_____ "average or acceptable" height		
_____ "average or acceptable" weight		
_____ English is your native language		
_____ Caucasian		
_____ European American		
_____ Christian		
_____ heterosexual		
_____ no physical disabilities		
_____ no mental disabilities		
_____ male		
_____ under 40 years old		
_____ "average or above" intelligence		
_____ above-average household income		
_____ post-secondary education		
_____ household in upper income neighborhood		
_____ right handed		

Activity 1.15

All class members should stand in the center of the room.

1. Listen to the following statements. For each, take either a step forward (+) or backward (-) depending on the instruction and your response to the statement.

   - In high school, you had a computer in the home where you lived. (+)

   - You have a computer where you live now. (+)

   - Your parents or other family members are partially or totally supporting your college education. (+)

   - You have access to the money you need when you have extra school expenses, such as books, supplies, etc. (+)

   - Your high school library was electronic (versus using card catalogues). (+)

   - You have two parents (one of each gender). (+)

   - One or more of your grandparents went to college. (+)

   - One or both of your parents went to college. (+)

   - One or more of your grandparents went to the college you are attending. (+)

   - One or both of your parents went to the college you are attending. (+)

   - You have one or more siblings who attend or attended college. (+)

   - You have one or more siblings who attend or attended the college you are attending. (+)

   - You have a trust fund. (+)

   - You have purchased a new piece of clothing in the last month. (+)

   - One or both of your parents can help you professionally with your job search after graduation. (+)

   - One or both of your parents have friends or business associates who can help you professionally with your job search after graduation. (+)

   - You attended summer orientation the summer before your first year of college. (+)

   - One or both of your parents attended summer orientation with you. (+)

   - In high school, you were enrolled in college preparation classes. (+)

   - You have access to a credit card. (+)

   - In high school, you had assistance from parents in locating information about colleges. (+)

Activity 1.15, continued

- ◆ You had to refrain from some sports activities in high school becuase of the cost. (–)

- ◆ You were unable to work at a popular location because you had no transportation of your own. (–)

- ◆ In high school, you had assistance from parents in completing application materials. (+)

- ◆ You had access to a car in high school. (+)

- ◆ Your car in high school was specifically purchased for you, not a family hand-me-down. (+)

- ◆ Before college, your parents regularly helped you with your homework or class projects. (+)

- ◆ In your K-12 school years, one or both of your parents were regularly involved in your school and communicating with your teachers. (+)

- ◆ In high school, one or both of your parents often proofread your papers. (+)

- ◆ In your family, you were expected to attend college. (+)

- ◆ One or both of your parents have what you would call a "high status" job. (+)

- ◆ You have traveled outside of North America. (+)

- ◆ You are fluent in more than one language. (+)

- ◆ You have a part-time job to pay for essential school or living expenses (not just spending money). (–)

- ◆ In high school, a counselor or teacher advised you to take vocational courses rather than college preparation courses. (–)

- ◆ You will be the first person in your immediate family to graduate from college. (–)

- ◆ You have been discouraged from pursuing an activity or field of study because of your gender. (–)

- ◆ You have been discouraged from pursuing an activity or field of study because of your race or ethnicity. (–)

- ◆ In high school, you were discouraged from taking certain courses because of your gender. (–)

- ◆ In high school, you were discouraged from taking certain courses because of your race. (–)

- ◆ You have been "steered away" from certain careers because of your sexual orientation. (–)

2. Look around the room to see how students are spread out or clustered.

3. What do the questions you were asked say about your privilege?

Examples: Impact of Dominant Privilege

You register your daughter in a preschool. The class roster includes the names, addresses and phone numbers of each child's family.

Privileged groups: Two-parent families (one male and one female); family that lives in "good" neighborhood

Nonprivileged groups: Single-parent, same-sex parents, children in foster care or living with grandparents or other nonparental caregivers, people living in stigmatized neighborhoods, people without telephones *(possible impact: physical risk, harassment, stereotyping; inequitable treatment for child)*

You are starting your career in a major company. Your work team, including your supervisor, agrees to meet regularly on Saturdays during the busy season that lasts about three months a year.

Privileged groups: Those without family responsibilities that prevent weekend work, those with religions that allow for Saturday work

Nonprivileged groups: Those with child care, elder care or other family issues, people with limited transportation, people with religious conflicts (e.g., Jewish people) *(possible impact: loss of job, appearing difficult to work with or less committed than others)*

Examples: Dominant Privilege

Example #1
An openly gay student repeatedly gets asked questions like, "When did you realize you were homosexual?" "How do you know you aren't heterosexual if you haven't tried it?" and "Do you think being gay is just a phase you are going through?"

Example #2
A Christian student makes repeated efforts to convert her Jewish roommate to Catholicism. The Christian student is concerned that her roommate will go to hell if she remains Jewish. There are very few Jewish students on campus, and the nearest synagogue is in a nearby city about an hour from campus. The Jewish student does not have a car.

Example #3
A student who requires use of an elevator is consistently five minutes late for class. The homework assignment and introduction to the important points for the day are given by the instructor during the first five minutes.

Example #4
A White mother in a grocery store has a hungry toddler in the cart. She feeds the child a few unweighed grapes. The produce manager sees the scene and smiles at the mother.

Example #5
A left-handed student is told he is required to use a spiral-bound notebook in class. The student usually chooses to use loose-leaf notebook paper because the spiral binding of other notebooks gets in the way of his left hand.

Example #6
A university is about to go to a system of accepting *only* online applications.

ACTIVITY 1.16

Use the preceding examples to think about the following.

1. In your own life, what identity privileges do you have and what privileges don't you have? How have these affected your everyday life?

2. How is dominant privilege part of each of the preceding examples?

3. What is the impact of privilege on nondominant (nonprivileged) groups?

4. What is the impact of privilege on dominant (privileged) groups?

5. How might the interactions in the examples be different if the people involved understood dominant privilege?

6. What are some other examples you have seen that illustrate privilege?

ACTIVITY 1.17

1. Using types of diversity, list groups that have dominant privilege in your university (e.g., traditional-age students).

2. Give two examples for each of your answers in the previous question of how the dominant group is advantaged.

3. Give two examples for each of your answers in the previous question of how the nondominant group is disadvantaged.

Examples: Profiling

Example #1
An employee follows a high-school student around a video store.

Example #2
Five African-American college students decide to attend an event in a nearby city. They discuss who will drive, and decide it should be the lightest-skinned female. She puts her hair in pigtails and they drive to the city without incident.

Example #3
On the way home from the event, an African-American male drives. Although he is driving the speed limit, the police stop them three times. Upon returning home, they joke about being guilty of "DWB."

Example #4
The number of Asian-American scientists targeted for investigations related to violations of national security are disproportionately high compared to European-American scientists.

ACTIVITY 1.18

Use the preceding example to respond to the following.

1. What is DWB?

2. What are the issues of privilege in the examples?

3. List the negatives about racial profiling or profiling based on age.

4. Discuss situations where you feel profiling (of any type) might be justified.

(Note to Instructor: See Instructor's Guide.)

ACTIVITY 1.19

1. What are examples of national issues and current events related to dominant privilege?

2. What are examples of global issues and current events related to dominant privilege?

ACTIVITY **1.20**

1. The following are common comments. Describe how each might reflect a dominant privilege perspective.

   ◆ Why is there a major for Women's Studies and not one for Men's Studies?

   ◆ Why can't people just get along?

   ◆ Why is a Black History Month necessary? Why don't other groups have months,
     too? Where do we draw the line?

   ◆ Why do gay people need to have organizations, rallies and parades? Shouldn't sexu-
     ality be private?

   ◆ Why do all of the Black students always hang out together?

2. List other comments that you have heard that reflect dominant privilege.

Levels of Acceptance of Difference: Intolerance, Tolerance and Authentic Acceptance

One way to view the range of behaviors that represent responses to diversity is to explore a continuum of levels of acceptance. While there are many levels and variations based on each situation or interaction being examined, three levels are included in this discussion: intolerance (nonacceptance), tolerance (limited or conditional acceptance, insincere appearance of acceptance) and authentic acceptance. In the continuum, intolerance and tolerance are not ideal—authentic acceptance is a goal. Using the three concepts to examine diversity interactions can raise awareness about one's own behaviors and the impact of those behaviors on others.

INTOLERANCE

When people think about racism, sexism, homophobia and other forms of discrimination, the most prominent examples are those of intolerance. The words and actions of hate groups, such as murder, cross-burning, verbal harassment and vandalism of churches and private property are examples of behaviors that illustrate intolerance. Intolerance is often blatant and unmistakable. For example, cases of physical harm to a person or property are usually considered to be intolerant behavior.

TOLERANCE

There are two reasons why the idea of "tolerance" may be difficult to understand. First, in everyday English, "tolerance" can have a positive connotation (e.g., "If only people could just be more tolerant of each other.") It can also be more negative (e.g., "Your father and I have tolerated that behavior long enough.") In the context of this discussion, tolerance is closer to "enduring" or "putting up with" in meaning. Tolerating a difference or behavior is not the same as accepting the difference or behavior.

Second, people often view issues as dichotomous rather than multidimensional. Using words and phrases like "pro" and "con," "on the other hand," and "both sides" often mask or minimize complexities of issues. In studying situations of bias and discrimination, a belief in dichotomies forces people to choose between intolerance and acceptance. A perspective on an issue of difference must be either "right or wrong" or "good and bad." Therefore, tolerance—a concept that can represent many levels between "intolerance" and "authentic acceptance"—can be difficult to grasp.

Tolerance is more subtle, passive, pervasive and complex than intolerance. It probably represents the majority of behaviors that are racist, sexist, homophobic, ableist or biased on some other type of diversity. Surface or conditional acceptance is often a part of tolerance. Other dimensions of tolerance may include the following.

◆ Tolerance is often based on ethnocentric views of superiority.
◆ The person who is "tolerating" (exhibiting the bias) does not believe their behavior is biased.
◆ The bias may not be obvious to those outside of the person or group being "tolerated."
◆ The bias is usually apparent to the person or group being "tolerated."
◆ "Tolerance" is likely to result in psychological or economic harm rather than physical harm.
◆ A person who is "tolerating" someone else is likely to deny it if challenged. For example, "I didn't mean anything by it," "I'm not prejudiced," or "I treat him just like I treat everyone else" are common responses.

AUTHENTIC ACCEPTANCE

Acceptance represents a true positive response to a person or group. Acceptance may be achieved when a person goes beyond *awareness* of a difference to *understanding* the difference. Authentic acceptance means that a person can value a behavior or characteristic different from one's own as equally valid or appropriate.

Understanding the difference between tolerance and authentic acceptance is an essential prerequisite to acceptance of differences. The following example and activities are designed to help you explore your own views about levels of acceptance.

Example: Levels of Acceptance

A female college student is playing an early morning golf game with three of her male friends. They have several holes left in the game when the club's golf professional approaches them. He informs the group that only males are allowed on the course between 9 a.m. and 5 p.m. that day, and since it is now 9 a.m., the female will have to leave the game. The males in the group laugh and tease the female about how they lucked out since her score was the best in the group. Reluctant to ruin the game for everyone, she laughs along and agrees to leave the game and wait for her friends in the clubhouse. Later, she is deeply conflicted by her desire to "not make a big deal about it" and her feelings about her friends' lack of support and trivialization of the incident.

ACTIVITY 1.21

1. If you are female, how would you have reacted and felt if you were the female golfer? If you are male, how do you think you might have reacted and felt if you were one of the males golfers?

2. What are other ways the males could have reacted? What are other ways the female could have reacted?

3. Discuss the levels of acceptance (intolerance, tolerance or authentic acceptance) by each of the following:

   a. the female student

   b. the male friends

   c. the golf professional

4. Think of an example of when you felt intolerance or tolerance by another person or group. Describe the situation and how you felt. Do you think the incident was intentional on the part of the other person or group? How did the intent affect your feelings? How did intent affect your response? Would your response be different if the situation happened again?

Activity 1.22

Using "I" for intolerance, "T" for tolerance and "A" for authentic acceptance, indicate which acceptance level you think each of the following scenarios represents. For each, write a rationale for your decision.

_____Responding to a racist comment by saying "But the person didn't mean anything by it."

_____An elementary school student teacher takes total responsibility for the class when the cooperating teacher becomes ill. The principal tells the student teacher "Since you are a male, we will do this. We would not do it with a female student teacher."

_____A White driver locks the doors of the car when driving through a predominantly Black neighborhood

_____In a television episode about gays in the series "Seinfeld," a recurring punchline is ". . . not that there is anything wrong with that."

_____A professor is talking to a "branch" campus student. When the professor learns that the student is from a regional campus, he asks the student if she will be able to thoroughly complete the work on time.

_____An apartment manager tells a White applicant for an apartment about churches and schools in the neighborhood. The same apartment manager tells a Mexican-American applicant that the terms of the lease will be strictly enforced.

_____When racial profiling is being discussed, a person says "But the reason profiling exists is because the people in that group are more likely to commit crimes."

_____A Black doctor in an emergency room is asked by a Black patient, "Can I see a White doctor instead?"

_____A fifth-grade student with a learning disability is called "dummy" by several classmates. The teacher ignores the comments, believing that they represent typical preadolescent behavior.

_____An application for a job requires a current address and whether the applicant owns or rents his or her home.

_____A female tells a joke about men being hesitant to ask for directions when lost.

Marginalization

A common consequence of dominant privilege is the marginalization of individuals or groups. When an individual or group is marginalized, the perspectives of the person or group are considered to be less important than the voices of others. The perspectives are often discounted completely, or given limited attention by those with more power.

Marginalization can occur because of gender, race, ethnicity, class, religion, ability level or other types of diversity. In addition to dominant privilege, it is connected to many of the concepts discussed in this chapter, such as bias, stereotyping, ethnocentrism and tolerance. The presence of those concepts can create a climate for marginalization by giving individuals or groups power over others.

Group marginalization is at the core of many issues and events. For example, in the United States presidential election of 2000, there were widely publicized accusations of marginalization of Black voters, including disproportionate numbers of Black voters who were turned away at the polls or whose votes were thrown away. Laws banning gay marriage marginalize gay couples by denying them legal and economic rights granted to heterosexual couples. Perceptions about limitations of disability and physical barriers in the architectural environment marginalize people who use wheelchairs.

The consequences of group marginalization are felt at a societal or global level, and often have systemic political, economic or legal consequences. Marginalization of individuals can also have psychological consequences.

ACTIVITY 1.23

1. Describe an example of when you felt marginalized. Why did you feel marginalized? What were the consequences?

2. Describe a current diversity-related local or national issue. How is marginalization a factor in the issue? What are the consequences of the marginalization?

3. Describe a current diversity-related global issue. How is marginalization a factor in the issue? What are the consequences of the marginalization?

Relationship of Diversity to Culture and Multiculturalism

Culture is often viewed as the behaviors, beliefs, values and attitudes of various groups. Broadly defined, culture can be defined as the way things are done within any group. Social constructionism as a basis for culture reflects the idea that culture is constructed and learned from social practices and historical contexts. Culture then ". . . appears to be 'natural,' or 'the way things are.' For example, the idea that women 'naturally' like to do housework is a social construction because this idea appears 'natural' due to its historical repetition, rather than it being 'true' in any essential sense." (Source: University of Maryland Diversity Dictionary at *www.inform.umd.edu/EdRes/Topic/Diversity/Reference/divdic.html*).

An important point in social construction-ism is that while culture is learned, it can be unlearned and then acted upon accordingly. The process of "unlearning" is dependent on both awareness of how culture is constructed, and an awareness of the benefits and limitations to any given behavior, belief, value or attitude.

A culture may be defined by geography, such as the culture of a country or region with-in a country. Neighborhood distinctions within a community often exist. Culture may also be influenced and defined by race, ethnicity, reli-gion or any type of diversity.

Cultures may apply to characteristics of spe-cific institutions or businesses. For example, a university culture may include characteristics that are common to other universities, and char-acteristics that are unique to that institution. Most—if not all—universities are designed to educate students, but the unique characteristics will be determined by the demographics of the student population (e.g., a "branch" campus) and the focus of the institution and strength of its programs (e.g., a military academy), among other things.

Multiculturalism is when people of different cultures are interacting within the context of a group, business, community or society. Defining types of diversity broadly suggests that multiple diversities are in place in every inter-action between people, and that each person represents diversity on many levels. Multi-culturalism usually refers to major categories of difference, such as race, ethnicity or religion. Level of multicultural competence refers to how effectively an individual or organization works with a variety of cultures.

ACTIVITY 1.24

1. If your college or university system were based on your values, what would it look like?

2. Describe your university in one sentence. Each student will then read his or her sentence aloud. During the reading, note the common patterns in the sentences. From the com-mon patterns, identify some elements of culture.

3. On what characteristics does your university share a common culture with other univer-sities in the state?

4. On what characteristics does your university differ from other universities in the state?

5. List five other examples of social constructionism. What are the underlying values for each of the examples?

6. How is social contructionism related to ethnocentrism?

Relationship of Diversity to Assimilation, Acculturation and Cultural Pluralism

Assimilation and acculturation are related to how people from a nondominant culture integrate into a dominant culture. Assimilation is when a group takes on the characteristics of the dominant culture, losing most of the char-acteristics of the original culture. Often people in the United States who are descended from immigrant groups consider themselves to be only "American," and have little knowledge or understanding of their cultural origin. The United States has been referred to as a "melting pot"—a term that acknowledges the role of assimilation in the history of the country.

There are many examples of attempts to involuntarily assimilate groups in the United States. For example, many Native American Indian children were sent to boarding schools that were often joyless and dismal places designed to break cultural and family ties. Another example was the common practice on Ellis Island of changing the names of immigrants upon arrival in the United States. Names were often changed to more "Americanized" versions simply to ease pronunciation.

One characteristic of a "melting pot" is that the original ingredients are still there. Many characteristics that are labeled as "generic American" are part of a racial or ethnic heritage, but have been made culturally invisible over time. When the origins of cultural elements are visible, they serve to enhance the cultural valuing of the source.

Acculturation is when a group takes on some of the characteristics of the dominant culture, while maintaining elements of their own culture. For example, ethnic neighborhoods in many cities often continue strong traditional ties to their culture, even through several generations. The reference to the United States as a "salad bowl" illustrates a shift to an acknowledgment of

Example: An Assimilation Story

When I was a young child, I remember seeing my great-grandmother sitting in the window seat of the dining room in my grandparents' farm house. She was my grandfather's mother, and she lived with my grandparents for several years before she died at age 96. She would sit in the window seat for hours, knitting scarves and looking outside at the expanse of white snow, plowed fields, and brightly painted red farm buildings, including a traditional barn, chicken coop and grain silo. The south-facing window seat provided the warmest and sunniest spot in the house during the long cold Iowa winters, when the Canadian winds would rip through the Plains states. I remember the sunlight hitting her straight white hair, which was always neatly combed in a bun on top of her head. She was very petite, probably around 5 feet tall and not more than 100 pounds. She rarely spoke to me, but occasionally scolded my younger brother when he would take candy from her dresser drawer. Although her scolding was in Swedish, which was her native language, my brother got the message, even though he was only three or four years old at the time.

My grandfather never talked to me about his Swedish heritage. My father had been taught little about the culture, with the exception of learning to count to ten in Swedish as a child. Most of the neighboring farmers were second-generation immigrants like my grandfather, but not Swedish. They came from many countries in Europe, and their culture (everyday life) in the United States was built on farming, not country of origin. A church and a grain elevator dominated the nearby small town. It looked like hundreds of other small towns in the rural middle United States—there was little in the built environment to represent the immigrant cultures. Instead, the town represented complete assimilation, and the desire of the first generation immigrants to succeed in their new country and to make a better life for their children—a life as "Americans." A primary criterion for being an American was to fit in and not be different.

I wish I had made an effort to ask my father before he died to teach my daughter Brenna to count to ten in Swedish. I wish there were more things we could teach her about the culture of her great-great grandmother—a culture of which Brenna is a product and with which she shares a heritage.

the value of acculturation, as well as maintaining more visible signs of the original culture.

Assimilation relates to the "blending in" behavior of a specific group within a dominant culture. In acculturation, a group can maintain elements of its culture, but remain separate or isolated from the dominant cultural group.

Cultural pluralism, on the other hand, relates to the culture as a whole, including the dominant cultural group or groups. In a pluralistic culture, there is mutual respect and acceptance among the component cultures. There is a common culture and elements of individual cultural heritages.

Example: An Acculturation Story

Each May, thousands of tulips bloom in Pella, Iowa. A three-day festival is the culmination of the year-round work of hundreds of residents of this small rural town. Houses throughout the town exhibit the Dutch heritage of the residents through the architecture and the neatly landscaped gardens. Pride of ownership is evident and, although everything is at its best for the festival, it is clear that this is a well-maintained town throughout the year. In the museum near the town center, pictures of each annual tulip queen for many decades give a picture of the values of the community and a continuity of life that a shared culture supports. Many of the young women in the pictures undoubtedly continue to live their lives in the community.

The museum also houses many artifacts from the community's history. Unlike many museums, where the exhibits represent a past that is barely recognizable in its connection to the present, the exhibits in this museum are strongly connected to the present. Black and white pictures show buildings that are still standing and a main street that is still the primary shopping district for the community. The names of people in the picture are family names that can still be found in the local telephone book. Household items, particularly garden tools, are identical to those still being used by the residents on the well-manicured streets outside the museum.

There are places like Pella all over the country. They may have apples or honey or dulcimers or chili or smelt instead of tulips, but the heritage and cultural traditions have prevailed. Connecting the places and the practices of the present to the past is an important prerequisite to understanding diversity.

ACTIVITY 1.25

1. What are the differences between the two previous examples? Why do you think assimilation dominated in one example and acculturation and cultural pluralism in the other?

2. Write a short story (three or four paragraphs) of an example of assimilation or acculturation from your own life. After completing the story, read it to identify underlying values. List the values inherent in the story. Also, discuss how your example reflects (or does not reflect) cultural pluralism.

3. What values are represented in the example about Pella, Iowa (e.g., pride in community and heritage)?

4. Describe festivals or other cultural activities in your community. How are the festivals or activities related to cultural assimilation, acculturation or pluralism?

ACTIVITY 1.26

1. What are examples of cultural groups that have assimilated in the United States? Why did they assimilate?

2. What is an example of a cultural group that has acculturated in the United States but has not achieved cultural pluralism? Why and how did they acculturate?

3. What is an example of a cultural group that has acculturated in the United States that has achieved cultural pluralism? Why and how did they acculturate?

4. What are some examples of current assimilation/acculturation challenges in the United States?

5. What are some examples of current assimilation and acculturation challenges globally?

6. In your opinion, what is ideal for the United States—cultural assimilation, acculturation or pluralism? Discuss why you feel the way you do.

ACTIVITY 1.27

(Adapted from Kitty Locker's *Business and Administrative Communication*, 5th edition, ©2000, Irwin/McGraw-Hill)

1. The following terms are often used to refer to the concepts of cultural assimilation, acculturation or pluralism. For each, describe the positive and negative connotations.

	Positive	Negative
❖ Melting pot		
❖ Salad bar		
❖ Stew		
❖ V-8		
❖ Crazy quilt		
❖ Tapestry		
❖ Tributaries		
❖ Mosaic		
❖ Symphony		

2. What other terms can you add that refer to cultural assimilation, acculturation or pluralism?

Major Categories of Diversity

"Two months ago I had a nice six-room apartment in Chicago. I had a good job. I had a son. When something happens to Negroes in the South, I said, 'that's their business, not mine.' Now I know how wrong I was. The death of my son has shown me what happens to any of us, anywhere in the world, had better be the business of all of us."

Mamie Bradley Till, mother of 14-year old Emmett Till, who was murdered in Mississippi in 1955 for whistling at a White woman

"Ism: Power plus prejudice."

From Diversity Glossary, General Electric Commercial Distribution Finance

Objectives of Chapter 2

The overall objective of Chapter 2 is to explore key concepts in major types of diversity and to continue to begin to explore types of diversity at a personal level. Specific objectives for Chapter 2 follow.

❖ Identify key concepts in socio-economic status and class diversities
❖ Examine age diversity
❖ Explore geographic diversities
❖ Learn about disability diversities
❖ Identify key concepts in race, skin color and ethnicity diversities
❖ Examine religious diversities
❖ Identify key concepts in gender and sexual orientation diversities
❖ Explore interrelationships between types of diversity (e.g., race, skin color and ethnicity)

Introduction

As discussed in the previous chapter, we are all diverse in many ways. The reasons for individual diversity include many factors, such as personality, the beliefs of one's parents and other family members, the influence of friends, music, television, race and ethnicity, among others. This chapter will further explore major dimensions of diversity.

Exploring how you are diverse provides insight in several ways. First, it can help you more consciously identify your own beliefs, attitudes and behaviors. Since our beliefs, attitudes and behaviors seem natural to us, we think of them as normal and anything different is often perceived as unusual, uncomfortable or even wrong. For example, if you live in a residence hall or work in an office it may seem natural to you to leave your door open during certain times of the day. For someone else, it might be more natural to keep the door closed.

Second, exploring how you are diverse can help you identify why you hold various beliefs. Forcing yourself to examine why you believe what you do gives you an opportunity to think about the reasons for diversity at a personal level.

Third, exploring your diversity can help you explore how you are different from or similar to others. We often gravitate toward people whom we perceive as similar to us. Inherent in that is a missed opportunity for expanded knowledge from difference.

Fourth, exploring your diversity can help you gain insight into how and why others may be different from or similar to you. Understanding the how and why of difference is an important prerequisite to analysis of diversity issues at many levels—individual, national and global.

Dimensions of Major Diversity Classifications

Looking at multiple diversity is complex. As discussed in Chapter 1, there are many types of diversity. This section focuses briefly on several of the major types of diversity. Each type of diversity listed is the source of considerable study in many academic fields. Our brief discussion in this chapter is not meant to provide depth of understanding. Rather, the discussion will introduce some of the central concepts in each type of diversity that are critical to exploring awareness, understanding and application of diversity concepts. Each dimension will be explored in more detail in later chapters.

Socio-Economic Status (or Class)

Socio-economic status is a highly complex concept with varying definitions within social sciences and other academic disciplines. For purposes of understanding diversity, in this book socio-economic status and class will be used interchangeably.

In the context of understanding diversity in the United States, both terms often refer to perceptions and stereotypes by others, rather than actual income, education or occupation. The multimillionaire with a high school education, who lives simply and has a "low-status" occupation, is likely to be perceived as being in a "lower" class than a medical doctor who has extensive debt. Labels such as "blue collar" and "white collar" are used to indicate occupation status.

There is often a perception in the United States that anyone can succeed (e.g., move "up" in class) if he or she tries hard enough. This belief is based in part on the experiences of early European immigrants who had considerable access to land and other resources. The belief that anyone can still succeed often shapes views about immigration policy, welfare policies and poverty, among others. It does not take societal barriers, differential treatment and unequal opportunity into account.

Globally, there are many variations of how class is defined. Often, lineage is critical in determining class, which in turn is highly related to status in society. For example, in India the caste system is highly structured.

ACTIVITY 2.1

1. Consider ways the family you grew up in was "classed." What impact has this had on your life, education, etc.?

2. List adjectives that describe "high class" and "low class."

3. When you meet someone, what are indicators of "class"?

4. What is inherent in language like "high class" and "low class" that is potentially stereotyping?

5. In relation to class, how does the experience of early European immigrants differ from the experience of current immigrants in the United States?

GEOGRAPHIC DIVERSITY

Geographic diversity is often used in the United States to generalize about class, status, race, ethnicity or other forms of diversity. In the United States, there are often strong ties between status and neighborhood. Within local communities, distinctions between the status of neighborhoods are often subtle and known only to residents. Phrases like "from the wrong side of the tracks" and the real estate adage "location, location, location" illustrate the important relationship of neighborhood to status in the United States.

Nationally, there are perceptions and stereotypes about states and regions. States that have size, population, and/or tourism are more likely to have national stereotypes. Examples are California, New York, Florida and Texas.

Regions also have stereotypes (e.g., New England, South, Midwest, West).

Perceptions about other countries are often based on level of familiarity and comparisons with one's own culture. Level of familiarity is often related to ethnic roots. For example, European traditions, cultural patterns and architecture may seem more comfortable for people in the United States who are descended from European immigrants.

Comparisons with one's own culture are often used in perceptions about geographic diversity. For example, the common use of the phrase "Third World" to refer to nonindustrialized countries illustrates an implied hierarchy—that industrialized countries are superior to those that are not industrialized.

Activity 2.2

1. Using the community where you grew up, describe a "good" neighborhood within the community. Describe a "bad" neighborhood.

2. How specifically were the neighborhoods distinguished in your community?

3. Could someone unfamiliar with the community make the same distinctions you did about "good" and "bad"? Why or why not?

4. What are stereotypes about certain states? (Specify states)

5. What are stereotypes about regions within the United States? (Specify regions)

6. What are stereotypes about countries? (Specify countries)

Example: Geographic Diversity

In the cities, villages and rural landscapes of Malta, a small country in the Mediterranean south of Sicily and east of Northern African, typical southern European streetscapes are seen. In the cities, grand and modest houses sit side by side, and are often indistinguishable on the outside. In cities and villages, houses are very near the street, often with only a narrow sidewalk separating the house from the street. There is no green space. In the urban parts of the island, just a street often separates towns. The Maltese people know where one town ends and another begins—outsiders do not.

Activity 2.3

Use the preceding example to respond to the following.

1. Is the status of your college related to its location?

2. How do you show status in the space where you currently live?

3. How does your culture show status with space?

4. Although it is probably different from your culture, speculate about how you think the Maltese show status with space.

5. Why do you think there are differences in use of space to show status by cultures?

6. Using the differences you have discussed, how can cultures be misinterpreted by differing perceptions about geographic diversity?

AGE

Perceptions about age vary widely around the world. In many cultures, people who are older are the most revered and considered to be the most wise and even envied.

In the United States, there are a number of historical and demographic trends that have affected perceptions of age, especially in certain ethnic cultures. Industrialization, movement from rural to more urban and suburban lifestyles and increased mobility and consequent separation of extended families have all led to shifts in perceptions of age.

The baby boom—a reference to the cohort of babies born between 1945 and 1960—has had a dramatic and continuing effect on perceptions of age and aging in the United States. Baby boomers have impacted culture by the presence of large numbers of people in their age categories. When they were born, hospital maternity wards were crowded. As boomers began school, schools were crowded. As they

---

ACTIVITY 2.4

1. At what age do you consider someone "old"?

2. What are the characteristics of an old person?

3. How many of the characteristics you listed were positive toward aging? How many were negative?

4. What are the implications of your views (e.g., how might people be stereotyped and discriminated against)?

5. What are some examples of how baby boomers are currently affecting popular culture?

6. Identify current issues in the United States that are related to ageism.

Example: Age

At a college campus located about 40 miles from a major city, the access road to the beltway around the city has a 45-mile-an-hour speed limit. The road, at one time nicknamed "The Highway to Heaven" because of narrow shoulders and a high number of fatal accidents, has few passing zones. Most people agree that from campus to downtown is about an hour trip, assuming traffic is moving smoothly. The road is a source of frustration for many people who use it. The following is one student's account of a recent trip.

"My girlfriend and I were late for meeting her father downtown for lunch. We left campus with about 30 minutes to get there. We got behind this old guy on the road. He was going 45 miles an hour and we couldn't pass him. He shouldn't have been driving. People who can't keep up should have their licenses taken away. We were late for lunch and my girlfriend's father was really ticked. It was the old guy's fault. The government should do something about people like him."

ACTIVITY 2.5

Use the preceding example to respond to the following.

1. Describe the perspectives of both drivers in the example.

2. Describe the ageism issues inherent in the example.

3. How are the ageism issues problematic for the young driver?

4. How are the ageism issues problematic for the older driver?

---

neared college age, college entrance became competitive. Then there was high demand for jobs and housing, as the boomers entered the work force.

In the 1960s and 1970s, when the baby boomers were teenagers and young adults, there was a strong youth culture, with slogans such as "Don't trust anyone over 30." Now the baby boomers are in middle age and nearing retirement age—a demographic that is likely to continue to impact cultural views on age and aging for the next several decades.

DISABILITY STATUS

Over six million people in the United States have a permanent disability (either physical or mental). In 1990, the Americans with Disabilities Act (ADA) was passed to prohibit discrimination in employment, transportation, and access to public facilities for people with disabilities. Provisions of the ADA and current issues related to both the ADA and other disability legislation will be discussed in greater depth in Chapter 8.

The civil rights movement of the 1960s led to a strong disability rights movement, particularly for people with physical disabilities in mobility, vision or hearing. The disability rights movement has attempted to reduce discrimination against people with disabilities through both legislation and awareness of disabilities.

Discrimination based on disability status can be a result of a variety of factors. There are often many perceptions and stereotypes about people with disabilities that can lead to discrimination. There are stereotypes about what the characteristics of a specific disability are, the effects of disabling conditions and the characteristics of people with disabilities, among others.

Discrimination against people with disabilities is sometimes based on erroneous notions of what it would cost to accommodate a disabled employee or what modifications would be necessary. Issues of equity, access and justice are often balanced with perceptions of economic cost issues.

Discrimination against people with disabilities can also be based on fear of litigation based on the ADA. Fear of litigation was inherent in the opposition to the ADA prior to its passage, and continues to be an issue for many, despite the fact that the ADA provisions are very broad and applied on a case-by-case basis.

As with other types of diversity (e.g., race, gender, religion), discrimination against people with disabilities in some cases may simply be based on a lack of awareness of disabilities, lack of exposure to people with disabilities and unfamiliarity with the issues involved. However, the negative consequences of the discrimination (no matter the intent) can be significant.

ACTIVITY 2.6

1. Draw yourself with a disability.

2. Draw yourself encountering a barrier.

3. Include other people in the picture. What are the people in the picture doing?

4. On the back of the picture, describe the disability you have. Be as specific as possible.

5. What does it feel like to imagine yourself with a disability?

6. Using your drawings, your instructor will ask you a series of questions that will be the basis for a class discussion.

(Note to instructor: See Instructor's Guide.)

RACE

Race is not a fixed biological concept. Race is a social construct that is defined from culture to culture and changes over time. For example, in the United States the definition of race historically distinguished English immigrants from other immigrants, Native American Indian people and Africans brought against their will to the United States. For example, in *A Different Mirror: A History of Multicultural America (1993)*, historian Ronald Takaki describes the English view of one group as ". . . lazy, 'naturally' given to 'idleness,' and unwilling to work for 'their own bread.' Dominated by 'innate sloth,' 'loose, barbarous and most wicked,' and living 'like beasts,' they were also thought to be criminals, an underclass inclined to steal from the English." (p. 27)

ACTIVITY 2.7

1. Who do you think the English were describing in the preceding Takaki passage? Why do you think that?

2. Your instructor will tell you what group was being described in the passage. Were you surprised? Why or why not?

3. How does the passage and description of the group change your view of how race is defined?

(Note to instructor: See Instructor's Guide.)

In the United States, race as a social construction has often been supported by laws. For example, most people are aware that during slavery, slaves were the property of their masters, and could be sold or disposed of at will. In 1809, long before the legal end to slavery, importation of slaves from Africa was halted. This meant that for slaveholders to increase their number of slaves, female slaves needed to be used as "breeders." The desire for more slaves, in addition to the rape of female slaves for sexual gratification, power, and control, led to considerable forced interbreeding of people from European and African descent over several generations. Post-slavery legislation often used the "one drop of blood rule"—that the presence of any African blood classified a person as Black under the law.

While some people proudly identify themselves as being biracial or multiracial, others see the terms as potentially problematic. First, "biracial" is often very narrowly used (e.g., for a person with one black and one white parent), when in reality many people in the United States could be considered to be multiracial based on historical definitions of race (e.g., biracial for one English and one Irish parent). Second, the terms "biracial" or "multiracial" may be used to label people, creating a perceived identity by others or to force the biracial person to "choose" an identity.

Legal segregation on the basis of race in employment, education, housing, use of public facilities and other services occurred until the passage of civil rights legislation in the 1960s. Even beyond the 1960s, interracial marriages were illegal in many states.

Legal definitions of race have been used for other groups as well. Currently, people with a specific percentage of Native American Indian her-

---

ACTIVITY 2.8

1. Consider your own racial and ethnic identity. Do you think the "one drop" concept applies to any parts of your racial or ethnic background? If not, think about how your identity would be affected if the "one drop" concept was applied to your ethnicity (e.g., one drop of German, one drop of Irish). How would labelling based on your ethnicity affect you (e.g., stereotypes about your ethnicity)?

2. How do common perceptions of race apply to you in the things that you do (e.g., school, work, sports)?

3. How do common perceptions of race apply to people who are biracial or multiracial? (Skip this question if you are biracial or multiracial and responded to question 2.)

4. Why have legal and societal barriers to interracial marriages between African Americans and European Americans been greater than between other groups?

5. How does race as a socially constructed concept affect perceptions about immigration?

6. How does race as a socially constructed concept affect issues in education, such as busing and admissions policies?

7. What are some other examples where race as a socially constructed concept affects national and global issues?

itage can qualify for certain legal rights, such as owning land on reservations. The percentage varies by Native American Indian tribe or nation.

There are at least two other important aspects of race that affect the awareness, understanding and application of diversity concepts. First, there is a link between the social construction of race and nearly every aspect of any society or culture. Race is implicit in all interactions.

Second, in social constructions of race, everyone has a race. However, people in the dominant race (such as Whites in the United States) often consider themselves "raceless." Such a construction perpetuates negatively comparing racial groups in the minority to those in the majority, or to an invisible construct. Everything other than "White" becomes an "other." (The term "othering" will be used as a verb throughout this book.) The notion of Whites as "raceless" also deprives some Whites the feeling of belonging to an ethnic group.

Example: Race

In a search to select a preschool for her daughter, a mother recently visited a popular local school that includes an intergenerational component with an adjacent long-term care facility for elderly residents. Encouraged by the school's interest in age as a component of diversity, the mother asked the director about the diversity of the students and staff on other characteristics, such as race, ethnicity, disability, and income level. The director focused her response on race and ethnicity. Clearly a bit uncomfortable, she apologetically reported that the school has not been successful in attracting students who were not White. She put it this way. "We can't seem to get those students. We only seem to get 'regular' [sic] students applying."

The director commented during the tour of the facility that the curriculum of the school included a strong component in history. As they looked at the February calendar of events for the classes, the mother asked the director if the school was doing anything for Black History Month. The director seemed a bit surprised and puzzled about why a White parent of a White child would be asking such a question. Her response was "No, we haven't done much with Black History Month yet."

Activity 2.9

1. In what ways is social construction of race apparent in the previous example?

2. In what ways was dominant privilege illustrated in the example?

3. What does the use of the phrase "regular students" imply?

4. In what ways do social constructions of race and dominant privilege "other" nondominant groups? ("Other" is used as a verb here.)

5. In what ways does focusing everything on their own norms disadvantage dominant racial groups?

The following activity is designed to help you explore the social construction of race and the effect of race on individuals and society by increasing your awareness of your personal early memories of racism or injustice. Early memories are useful in identifying aspects of social construction of race that seem normative to us as adults, but appeared confusing or unjust as children.

ACTIVITY 2.10

(Adapted from an activity described by Peggy McIntosh in a presentation at Miami University, February 1998)

1. Think about the first time you became aware of an aspect of difference between people (e.g., race, ethnicity). Write down some notes about the details of the event, including where you were, how old you were, what you were feeling and anything else that you remember.

2. Describe the event in first-person present tense (see the example below).

3. Reflect on how and why the event affected you, any dissonant feelings the event created, and how the dissonance was resolved.

Example:

I am with my parents visiting my aunt and uncle in Philadelphia. I am six years old. My aunt and uncle and I are in downtown Philadelphia for the afternoon. It is very different from anything I have ever seen as a child growing up in rural Iowa. The buildings are tall, and there are many, many people everywhere. The experience is exciting and scary at the same time. I notice a water feature in a nearby plaza. It is a beautiful circular reflecting pool with a large fountain in the middle. I have never seen anything like it. There are several children playing in the water. It is a warm summer day, and seeing the children my age playing draws me to the water. I ask my aunt and uncle if I can approach the pool. They look at each other uncomfortably and do not answer. I don't understand why, and ask again. My aunt says, "No, you can't play in the pool. Those are colored children. You can't play with them." I feel confused. I don't know what my aunt means by colored. I am colored—my skin is peach. They are colored—their skin is brown. How are they different, and why doesn't my aunt know I am colored, too?

DISCUSSION QUESTIONS:

1. As a class, discuss the age range of when the personal narrative examples occurred. What are the implications of that age range for understanding social construction of race?

2. As a class, discuss the strategies used by students to reduce the dissonance created by the events. What are options for reducing dissonance?

COLOR

Skin color is a diversity classification that may be related to race, class, ethnicity or religion. Color may be used to designate social class, as in the caste system in India. In rural areas of the United States, lighter skin colors among Whites historically were preferred because of the assumption that darker skin was associated with outdoor physical work. Ironically, having a suntan now may have the opposite interpretation, as a sign of leisure and wealth. Historically, lighter skin colors among Blacks were preferred also, as evidenced by the "paper bag test" and being called "high yellow." The paper bag test was whether a person was lighter or darker than the color of a brown paper bag. People who were "high yellow" had light, yellowish undertones to the skin color that were considered to be the most desirable.

In the mid-1990s, professional athlete O.J. Simpson was charged with the murders of his ex-wife Nicole Brown Simpson and Ron Goldman. The case received extensive media coverage. *Time* magazine ran a cover photograph of Simpson; *Time* was subsequently charged with darkening the skin tone of Simpson on the photograph to make him appear more sinister. The controversy that followed raised questions about skin-color bias in the United States.

Cases of discrimination involving skin color bias (colorism) have dramatically increased in recent years. (See Equal Employment Opportunity Commission website for most recent statistics.) In 2003, a Black employee won a discrimination case against his Black supervisor, who repeatedly made derogatory comments about his skin color. Other cases have involved Arab and Native American plaintiffs. It is expected that the increase in skin color discrimination cases will continue to grow as the demographics of the United States change from White, European American as the dominant racial group.

ACTIVITY 2.11

1. For a 24-hour period, focus on increasing awareness of skin color variations in the people around you. Keep a log of the people, their skin tones, the context (e.g., walking to class, sitting in a classroom, in a dining hall), and your reaction (e.g., comfort level).

2. Describe trends in your impressions. How did you react or feel when you were near people with certain skin colors? What do you think this means? Where did you learn to make the distinctions you made?

Example: Skin Color

In 1998, DNA evidence showed that Thomas Jefferson fathered at least one child (it is reported elsewhere that more likely he fathered as many as six children) by his slave Sally Hemming. During his candidacy for presidency, the long-term relationship between Hemming and Jefferson created a scandal in the campaign. It is thought that of the three children who survived to adulthood, one stayed within the African-American community, and two "passed as White" throughout their lives. Although the relationship to Jefferson was well known among the Hemming descendants and African Americans in general, mainstream historians discounted it until the DNA testing confirmed the relationship.

The Jefferson/Hemming case has led to renewed discussions about the meaning of race. The descendants of most Africans brought to the United States as slaves have different levels of European-American heritage, due to the rape of many females during slavery over several generations. It is likely that many slaves passed as White after being emancipated to avoid painful societal treatment, oppression and discrimination, thus increasing the likelihood that many descendants of European Americans have African heritage too.

In February 2000, a fictionalized television mini-series on the Jefferson/Hemming relationship aired. Following the broadcast, a local television station in Dayton, Ohio, interviewed a family of descendants. One of them, a young man in his late teens, reported that as a child all of the students in his class were asked to talk about their heritage. He proudly announced to the class that he was a descendent of Thomas Jefferson. He was promptly kicked out of class by his teacher and sent to the principal's office for discipline, since it was assumed by the teacher that he had to be lying.

ACTIVITY 2.12

Use the preceding example to answer the following questions.

1. Do you think you would have been kicked out of your elementary school class if you claimed you were a descendent of Thomas Jefferson? Why or why not?

2. What do you think motivated historians to keep the relationship between Thomas Jefferson and Sally Hemming a secret or even deny it? Who benefited? Who did not benefit?

3. What are some examples of where skin color is part of culture (e.g., fairy tales and nursery rhymes—". . . who's the fairest of them all?")

4. Consider your own skin color. Is it the same or different from others in your family? How does your skin color relate to your ethnicity? What are the implications of your skin color in society?

5. What are some national or global examples of events, issues or policies where skin color is a factor?

ETHNICITY

Ethnicity is related to many aspects of culture, including geography, religion, and learned social and moral traditions. Unlike race, which is socially constructed and variable over time, ethnicity can often (but not always) be more objectively identified. Ethnicity often refers to geographic origins related to countries or regions. For example, one's ethnic affiliation may be based on the countries one's ancestors came from.

Ethnicity sometimes corresponds with current definitions of race (e.g., most—but not all—Blacks in the United States have African heritage) and sometimes not (e.g., all Whites are not European). Ethnicity sometimes overlaps with religion, such as in the case of Judaism.

Many people in the United States can identify their ethnicity or ethnic origins easily. Others, particularly people whose ancestors immigrated or were brought to the United States several generations ago, have more difficulty in identifying ethnic origins. In either case, an awareness of personal ethnicity is an important prerequisite to understanding the impact of ethnicity on individuals and cultures.

ACTIVITY 2.13

1. How do you define your ethnicity?

2. If your first reaction is to define your ethnicity as "American," what does being an American mean to you? Be as specific as possible in your answer.

3. Trace the ethnic roots of your family. Define family as the adults (birth parent or parents, adopted parent or parents, etc.) who were your primary caregivers as a child. If you are fourth- or fifth-generation American, you might have multiple countries and cultures represented in your background. If possible, discuss your ethnicity with family members (e.g., parents, grandparents).

What do you know about each ethnic group?

What are the positive attributes (or stereotypes) about each group?

What are the negative attributes (or stereotypes) about each group?

4. Were there cultural conflicts in your family history, such as intermarrying between cultures or religions? How did those situations affect your family? How do you feel those situations affect you?

5. With which groups in your ethnicity do you most closely identify? Why? (In exploring why, you can examine whether your identification is based on percentage of your ethnicity, race, religion, your family, societal perceptions, etc.)

6. For those parts of your ethnicity that you do not closely identify, explore why.

7. Do cultural definitions or societal level of acceptance of race and ethnicity alter your choice in accepting or rejecting parts of your ethnicity (e.g., having European and/or African ethnicity)? Discuss the meaning of the level of choice you have.

RELIGION

Dominant world religions include Islam, Hinduism, Buddhism, Judaism and Christianity. Religion is often related to ethnicity and other aspects of culture. The following quote reprinted with permission from a student illustrates one person's description of that relationship in her life.

> *Judaism is understandably considered both a religion and an ethnicity. I do not consider myself a very religious person and although my faith has grown in the last few years, I identify more with the cultural connections that Judaism provides me than the religious ones. I embrace Judaism as my strongest and most prominent cultural link to all of my ancestors despite their varying nationalities. (Carrie Lewin, 2000)*

There are many examples of how religion affects national and global events and policies. In the United States, controversies about religion in schools and polygamous religious marriages are two examples. Many of the founding fathers in the United States were Presbyterian Protestants. The government structure that they created, therefore, was based on the structure of the Presbyterian Church.

Religious differences are also part of global conflicts, such as in Northern Ireland, Bosnia, and the Middle East. These conflicts often include complex historical relationships between religion and other aspects of culture. The United States war in Iraq has heightened awareness of world regions.

ACTIVITY 2.14

1. What is your religion?

2. Was your religion dominant in the community where you grew up? How did the dominance (or nondominance) affect you?

3. Are your religious beliefs dominant or nondominant at the university you are attending? How are they visible (e.g., vacations around Christian holidays rather than Muslim, Jewish holidays)? How does the dominance (or nondominance) affect you?

4. Are your religious beliefs dominant in the United States? How did the dominance (or nondominance) affect you?

5. How is your religion related to other types of diversity (e.g., your race, your ethnicity)?

6. What are examples of current local, national and global events related to religion?

GENDER

The roles of women and men vary tremendously from culture to culture. Historically, men in many cultures (including the United States) have had dominant power in many areas.

In the United States in the 1960s, the women's rights movement corresponded to the Civil Rights movement of other groups. In both movements, levels of awareness were raised about issues of bias and discrimination.

In the workplace, women in the United States currently make about 25 percent less money than men in comparable jobs. Another work-related concept is the "glass ceiling"—employment practices that prevent women from achieving high-level positions at the same rates as men.

Nationally, there are many issues related to women. Gender roles in families, workplace and child-care issues, reproductive rights, and women in the military are a few examples. These same issues affect men as well. For example, if women are entirely responsible for child rearing, men are denied the pleasures of children. If women are dependent on men, men are not allowed to show their vulnerability.

Globally, there are also many issues related to women. Examples include slavery in the Sudan and elsewhere, forced prostitution, the treatment of women in Afghanistan, and genital mutilation of women in many countries. On the other hand, there has still not been a woman president or vice-president in the United States; many other countries stereotyped as more sexist have had high-ranking female officials.

Issues that relate to gender roles for men often get less attention than those do for women, but exist nevertheless. Gender roles and expectations often constrain choices for men as well as women. An example from spring 2000 surrounds Tony Blair, the Prime Minister of England. His pregnant wife encouraged her husband to take a parental leave upon the birth of the child. The parental leave was new legislation; Prime Minister Blair was reluctant about taking the leave. Similarly, few men with parental leave options in the United States exercise those options.

ACTIVITY 2.15

1. What gender roles exist in your family? How are those gender roles similar or different from those of other families you know?

2. What are some implications of the gender roles in your family for both men and women?

3. What is your definition of "feminism"?

4. List and discuss some issues in the United States that are related to gender (in addition to those described above).

5. List and discuss some global issues that are related to gender (in addition to those described above).

6. How do perceptions of women and women's roles relate to each of the issues identified in the previous questions?

Examples: Gender

Example #1

A father is the primary caregiver for the two young children in the family. At the school one of the children attends, the female staff members consistently refuse to give the father information about upcoming events, requests for the parents to bring items to schools for parties, and dress codes for school pictures, among other things. Usually the staff member will say something like, "Have your wife call us" to the father.

Example #2

When women began to enter the broadcasting field in the 1970s as on-air personalities, the first woman in a local television market was the weather forecaster. The introductions at the top of the newscast went something like this. "Tonight, we have Jim Smith with the news, Joe Jones with the sports, and Connie with the weather."

Example #3

During a university meeting, introductions were made for three faculty who were receiving awards. The first male faculty had a Ph.D., and was introduced as Dr. Smith. The second male faculty did not have a Ph.D. and was introduced as Professor Jones. The female award recipient, who had a Ph.D., was introduced by her first and last name, without mention of her professional title. The subtle difference went unnoticed by most observers.

ACTIVITY 2.16

Use the preceding examples to respond to the following.

1. What values and beliefs about gender are represented in the previous examples?

2. In the previous examples, how does the subtle differential treatment of men and women affect perceptions about gender?

3. List other examples of situations where men and women are defined differently.

Gender Identity

Gender identity refers to how one thinks of oneself as masculine or feminine. It is a somewhat separate concept from sexual identity or orientation, which will be discussed in the next section. The societal view of gender identity is related to the presence of a penis (masculine) or a vagina (feminine). When people do not follow these societal views, they are often targeted for mistreatment and discrimination. (The murder of Brandon Teena, a Nebraska woman with a male identity, was the subject of an Academy Award winning movie "Boys Don't Cry").

There are many concepts related to gender identity. Some transgender-related terms include cross-dresser, female impersonator, transnatural, transsexual, and intersexual/intersected person. A cross-dresser wears clothing of the opposite sex, usually part-time. A female impersonator is a man dressed as a celebrity, usually for entertainment purposes. A transnatural is someone who identifies with the opposite sex, but opts to not have genital surgery. A transsexual is someone who has had genital surgery or hopes to have gender reassignment. An intersexual/intersected person is someone who was born with ambiguous genitalia. In many cases, gender was arbitrarily assigned at birth, often leading to gender identity issues.

SEXUAL IDENTITY

It is widely estimated that 10 percent of the population of the United States is homosexual. Similar to women's rights and disability rights, gay rights emerged from the civil rights movement.

Sexual identity relates to which gender one is sexually attracted to.

Some people believe that sexual identity is a choice; others believe it is a hereditary predisposition at birth. The choice or predisposition controversy is sometimes at the heart of opinions. Often people who believe being gay is wrong or can be changed believe in the choice origin theory. Recent medical research has begun to explore physiological determinants of sexual identity. People who are gay or accepting of gays often believe that sexual identity is not a choice that a person makes. That distinction is also reflected in language. "Sexual preference" implies choice. "Sexual orientation" is a more preferred term by many gays because it does not imply choice.

Legal protections for gays in the United States are considerably more limited than for people representing many other types of diversity. Although some hate crime legislation includes gays as a protected category of people, there are few employment or housing laws that make it illegal to discriminate on the basis of sexual identity. (Legal protections based on gender identity are limited, too.)

Although legal protections are still limited, there have recently been a number of state and local cases that have received considerable press. In 2000, Vermont was the first state to legalize same-sex civil unions. In November 2003, Massachusetts struck down a ban on same-sex marriages. In February 2004, gay marriages began to be performed in San Francisco, but California would not register the marriages. As of November 2003, 37 states have enacted "Defense of Marriage Acts" that ban same-sex marriage. Others will likely follow. In May 2004, Massachusetts began performing same-sex marriages.

At the National level, at the time of this writing President George W. Bush is endorsing a constitutional amendment that would restrict marriage to two people of the opposite sex, but leave open that states could allow civil unions. He cited the Massachusetts and San Francisco cases as the reason a constitutional amendment should be enacted. Both proponents and opponents of gay marriage are active in the debate about this amendment. Readers are urged to review updated information available through Internet and published news sources, since gay marriage is likely to be one of the most important new civil rights battles in the coming years.

ACTIVITY 2.17

1. Did you know the differences between gender identity and sexual identity before this reading?

2. What gender and sexual identities are accepted in your family? How do you know?

3. What gender and sexual identities do your friends accept? How do you know?

4. What treatment do you or would you be likely to experience by your family and friends as a person of homosexual or bisexual identity?

5. What are your opinions about why legal protections for gays are limited?

6. List and discuss some issues in the United States that are related to sexual orientation (e.g., gays in the military).

7. List and discuss some issues globally that are related to gender and sexual identities (e.g., religious perspectives).

Examples: Sexual Orientation

Example #1

Two male college students decided to hold a commitment ceremony on Gay Marriage Awareness Day. The ceremony was held in a local Episcopal Church and a Unitarian minister performed the service. The story of the ceremony, along with an accompanying picture of the couple, was published on the front page of the student newspaper.

Shortly after the story was published, it was anonymously sent to the parents of one of the students. The father of the student, previously unaware of his son's sexual orientation, threatened to end financial support for college.

Example #2

Bill is a 36-year-old male attending college to get his undergraduate degree. He also works full-time at a local factory. One of his coworkers is openly gay. Although they have become friends, Bill is conflicted about the friendship. While he has much in common with his friend, Bill does not believe being gay is normal or right. His views are based on his religious beliefs and what he learned from his family.

Example #3

In an undergraduate residence hall, several residents were angry with the hall adviser. During gay awareness week, they posted signs on his front door, implying he was gay. The signs were threatening and used a number of slurs about gays.

Many students in the residence hall thought that the adviser deserved the treatment because he was unpopular with his residents. Some felt that calling the adviser gay was simply a way to verbally attack him. Most did not think the labeling, slurs and threats were a big deal.

Example #4

The "uptown" area, or campus business and entertainment district, is busy on weekend nights with students. At around 11 p.m., a male student sees a friend across the street. To get the friends attention and greet him, he laughingly calls out "Hey, you faggot—what are you doing uptown?"

Example #5

A popular and well-respected teacher in a public high school is fired after people in the community learn the teacher is gay.

ACTIVITY 2.18

Use the preceding examples to answer the following questions.

1. What are the issues in the preceding examples?

2. What in society makes these examples common and accepted occurrences?

3. How are persons with gay or bisexual identities disadvantaged?

4. What are examples of gay issues on your campus or in your community?

CHAPTER 3

Why Awareness, Understanding and Application of Diversity Issues Are Important

"You must be the change you wish to see in the world."

Mahatma Gandhi

"As long as you keep a person down, some part of you has to be down there to hold him down, so it means you cannot soar as you otherwise might."

Marian Anderson, singer

Objectives of Chapter 3

The overall objective of Chapter 3 is to learn how a greater understanding of diversity concepts can benefit students in their personal and professional lives and as lifelong learners. Specific objectives for Chapter 3 follow.

❖ Explore personal motivation for understanding differences
❖ Identify how knowledge of diversity concepts can enhance interpersonal interactions, critical thinking and problem solving
❖ Identify how knowledge of diversity concepts can enhance understanding of current U. S. and world events
❖ Learn about changing demographic and immigration patterns in the United States
❖ Learn about global demographics
❖ Explore diversity concepts in interdisciplinary applications
❖ Explore diversity concepts within one's own major field of study

Personal Motivation for Understanding Difference

Why do some individuals feel that understanding diversity is important, while others do not? The personal motivations for understanding (or denying) differences are as diverse as people themselves. Contributing factors include previous experience with difference, perception of relevance of diversity issues, attitudes of family and friends and professional interests and career plans, among others.

There are both intrinsic and extrinsic reasons for understanding diversity. Using a classic advertising campaign as a metaphor, there are people who can be described as "I'd like to buy the world a Coke" people who are more likely to be motivated by intrinsic factors such as kindness and compassion. "I'd like to buy the world a Coke" people often are people-oriented and feel that awareness and understanding of diversity is important because of concerns for equity and social justice. People in fields such as education, social work and social sciences are often (but not always) in this category.

"I'd like to sell the world a Coke" people are more likely to be motivated by extrinsic factors such as bottom-line profit. "I'd like to sell the world a Coke" people may be interested in understanding diversity because of the market potential diverse people represent. Understanding diversity means understanding potential clients. People in fields such as business are often (but not always) in this category.

Sometimes people are motivated by a combination of factors. The following example illustrates a college-student perspective where both intrinsic and extrinsic factors were part of the thinking of the student.

Example: Diversity Motivation

An African-American male student on a predominantly White campus was attending a meeting for students with the Dean. At one point, the Dean asked the student why he chose the university. The student responded "I grew up in a Black neighborhood and went to predominantly Black schools. I need to be at a university like this one to better understand White people, since wherever I work after school will probably be mostly White. After I graduate, if something racial is going on in my workplace, I may get fired. In contrast, if something racial is going on in the workplace, my White colleagues will get diversity training."

ACTIVITY 3.1

1. How do you feel about the student's statement in the above example?

2. How is the perspective of the student in the previous example different from or similar to your perspective?

3. Describe your feelings about studying diversity. What factors do you believe have influenced your feelings?

4. Think about your own diversity motivation. Are you not motivated, intrinsically motivated ("I'd like to buy the world a Coke"), extrinsically motivated ("I'd like to sell the world a Coke") or a combination? Discuss your answer.

5. What are some concrete ways in which understanding diversity could assist you in your future career and in your personal goals?

Diversity as a Tool for Understanding Self and Others

Since many of our interactions are interpersonal, the importance of understanding diversity as a tool for understanding one's self and others in our lives has the potential for considerable impact. Understanding one's own diversity is an important prerequisite to understanding the diversity of others.

Especially when diversity is defined broadly to include individually variable characteristics such as communication styles, learning styles and negotiation styles, it is clear to see how a greater understanding of one's self can contribute to greater understanding of others. For example, greater understanding of difference can be key in conflict resolution, an inevitable result of interaction.

ACTIVITY 3.2

1. What skills and characteristics do you feel you bring to the study of diversity?

2. What skills and characteristics do you feel you will bring to the class in classroom discussions and group work?

3. How would you describe your style in handling differences of opinions with others?

Diversity as a Tool for Critical Thinking for Problem Solving

Critical thinking for problem solving includes awareness and understanding of multiple perspectives. Knowing the "what" of a situation is an important prerequisite to exploring the "why." Since diversity issues are usually complex and multidimensional, they provide excellent examples for in-depth analysis. On the other hand, it is that same complexity that makes it easier for people to stereotype or develop hasty opinions rather than to fully explore an issue. The content, examples and activities throughout this book will help students develop skills in analyzing complex diversity-related topics.

The skills developed using diversity examples can also be applied to critical thinking in any area. The "what" and "why" of a situation or challenge can be consciously examined, and can lead to application and synthesis. Specific diversity-related examples from a range of academic disciplines will be discussed later in this chapter.

Example: Barriers to Critical Thinking

On September 11, 2001, I was scheduled to teach a diversity class from 12:30–1:45 p.m. The morning had been filled with the news of the terrorist attacks in New York, Washington, D.C., and Pennsylvania. I was not sure what the class would be feeling, but it was clear to me that we needed to talk about the events of the day.

When I arrived in class, the students (like everyone else in the country) were confused, saddened and angry. No one in the class had friends or relatives at the attack sites, but a few students had friends who were concerned about the safety of loved ones.

Students wanted to talk about what was going on, and the conversation followed the path they wanted to take. Students assumed (although there was no evidence at that point, just a few hours after the attack) that the terrorists were "Middle Eastern" or "Arab." Many students felt that we (the United States) should go in and bomb everything in the Middle East. The consensus of the group was that we should go to war immediately.

One student in the class suggested we think about the perspectives of all involved. She asked questions like "What would lead people to do such a horrible thing?" and "How do we know for sure who did it?" Other students in the class attempted to shout her down, but she persisted in raising questions. Although her questions and comments were always prefaced with something like "This was an awful thing, and I acknowledge that" the other students began to accuse her of being sympathetic to the attackers and disloyal to the United States.

During the next meeting two days later, I took the opportunity to debrief what had happened in the previous class with the students. It was agreed that although the students were aware of the importance of being able to look at issues from multiple perspectives, the shock and grief had prevented them from doing so immediately after the event. The fact that they were unable even to allow someone to present alternate opinions that moved beyond the "what" to the "why" of the situation further highlighted the fact that the enormous impact of the event was a barrier to critical thinking.

ACTIVITY 3.3

1. What does "critical thinking" mean to you?

2. Think about the process that you used to select a university. What factors, issues and questions were included in the process you used?

3. How did you evaluate the criteria you used in selecting a university?

4. What issues of critical thinking are included in the other classes you are taking this term?

5. Identify an example of a complex decision you have made in your personal life. How did you use critical thinking in the process?

Diversity as a Tool for Understanding Implications of National and World Demographics

National and global demographics are useful for exploring diversity concepts in several ways. First, they serve as a starting point to compare characteristics of the United States and the world. Such a comparison is useful in exploring ethnocentrism, analyzing cultural differences and similarities and applying diversity to specific contexts, such as international business. Second, anticipating demographic trends within the United States can be used to increase awareness and understanding of groups whose populations are increasing, such as Hispanics. Third, demographics are helpful in understanding relationships of people to systems of culture (e.g., culture) and current issues (e.g., immigration).

CHANGING NATIONAL AND LOCAL DEMOGRAPHICS

The current population estimate (as of April 2004) for the United States is approximately 293 million people. The United States Bureau of the Census reports that in 2000 (the most recent data available) 81% of the United States population is White; 12.7% is Black; 3.7% is Asian and 2.5% is all other races (0.7% is Native American Indian, Eskimo or Aleut, not Hispanic) (www.census.gov).

Census data for Hispanic people are also reported separately from race because Hispanics can be any race. Most Hispanics in the United States are White. Slightly more than 30% of Whites are Hispanic.

According to census data, Blacks and Hispanics represented nearly equal numbers in the 2000 census. There were 35,818 million Blacks (representing 12.7% of the population) and 35,622 million Hispanics (representing 12.6% of the population).

Population projections through 2050 are also available from the U.S. Department of the Census, and those data show differences in projected growth rates in the Black and Hispanic populations in the United States. In 2010, for example, Blacks will be 13.1% of the population (only 0.4% higher than in 2000), and Hispanics will be 15.5% of the population (2.9% higher than in 2000). Projections for 2050 are that Blacks will be 14.5% of the population, and Hispanics will be 24.4% of the population.

In some states, such as Texas, California, New York and Florida, there are significant percentages of Hispanic or Latino(a) residents. In other states, there are pockets of immigration that are creating shifts in local communities. For example, in Arkansas, Nevada, North Carolina and Georgia, the Hispanic population more than doubled between 1990 and 1998 (U.S. Bureau of the Census).

In addition to national and state demographic changes, there are many examples of local shifts in the Hispanic population as well. Sudden local shifts due to changes in employment patterns, immigration or other factors often have considerable impact on communities. Those communities are frequently ill-equipped to handle such changes.

Example: Effects of Local Demographic Change

A community with a predominantly White population of around 100,000 people has little racial diversity. The largest cultural minority in the community is people from Appalachia who, because they are White, are often invisible in the community as a separate cultural entity.

Shifts in local industry have led to a labor shortage. Several hundred legal Mexican immigrants have been recruited to fill the jobs. Most are married with families. Because the jobs are not high paying, the immigrants have clustered in a few lower-middle-class neighborhoods. An elementary school in one of the neighborhoods that had one Spanish-speaking student the previous year has 60 Spanish-speaking students in the current academic year. Most of the teachers do not speak Spanish.

Some White neighbors in the areas where the Mexican immigrants live are complaining that the presence of Mexicans in the neighborhood is reducing property values and increasing crime. There is no basis for the complaint, but the story is covered by a local radio station. Only White residents are interviewed in the story, where one woman bitterly complains that her elderly mother is now afraid to leave the house.

ACTIVITY 3.4

1. What are the stereotypes about Mexicans in the previous example?

2. How did the local community perpetuate those stereotypes?

3. What could have been done to better prepare for demographic change and reduce the risk of cultural conflict?

4. What are the issues involved in the case of the elementary school?

WORLD DEMOGRAPHICS

Many of the dominant characteristics of the United States (e.g., race, religion) are minority characteristics globally. The following example illustrates that concept.

Example: Global Demographics

If we could shrink the earth's population to a village of precisely 100 people, with all the existing human ratios remaining the same, it would look something like the following.

There would be:

57 Asians

21 Europeans

14 from the Western Hemisphere, both North and South

8 Africans

30 would be White

70 would not be White

30 would be Christian

70 would not be Christian

89 would be heterosexual

11 would be homosexual

6 people would possess 59% of the entire world's wealth and all 6 would be from the United States

80 would live in substandard housing

70 would be unable to read

50 would suffer from malnutrition

1 would be near death

1 would be near birth

1 (yes, only one) would have a college education

1 would own a computer

Source: Phillip M. Harter, M.D. FACEP, Stanford University School of Medicine

---

ACTIVITY 3.5

1. Next to each category in the previous example, indicate whether you are in the minority or majority in the world.

2. Also indicate next to each category what it means to you to be in the minority or majority (a) as a college student and (b) in your future professional life.

Interdisciplinary Applications of Diversity Concepts

Given a broad definition of diversity, it is easy to see that there are diversity concepts in every academic discipline. Whether explicitly or implicitly acknowledged, diversity concepts are ever present; a conscious awareness of those concepts can enhance the study of any discipline.

Awareness of diversity concepts can also contribute to understanding of other disciplines. Many diversity concepts cross disciplinary boundaries. For example, the controversy over evolution versus creationism is an issue in both science and education because of differences in spiritual belief systems. The ethical issues of health and health care are included in nursing, medicine, physical training and dietetics, among others. Health care issues such as euthanasia, eating disorders and holistic medicine are just a few examples of interdisciplinary diversity-related health care issues.

Social Sciences

The social sciences offer many examples of how diversity and culture are explicitly part of the various disciplines. Sociology, anthropology, family studies, social work and psychology, among others, have obvious connections to diversity in their examination of differences and similarities between people and cultures. History, political science and economics all represent fields of study that focus on the major institutions of culture, both in the United States and globally.

For the purpose of illustration, the following discussion focuses on issues in history. However, any academic discipline within the social sciences could provide many examples that would be equally illustrative of diversity connections.

There are numerous examples of how the understanding of historical events has changed over time in the United States, particularly history involving people in nondominant cultures. The following is a list of a few examples from United States history.

♦ In 1921, a riot instigated by Whites in an affluent Black neighborhood in Tulsa, Oklahoma, resulted in the deaths of over 300 African Americans. An investigation in 2000 led to considerable national attention. History books typically only discuss rioting by persons from minority populations, giving readers a particular impression based on race.

♦ In World War II, thousands of Japanese Americans were held in internment camps in several states from California to Arkansas. The economic and psychological damage to individuals and families was extensive. History books often discuss this type of population treatment in other countries but not in the United States.

♦ For 40 years in the 20th century, nearly 400 African-American men in Tuskegee, Alabama, were involved without their knowledge in an experiment to study the effects of syphilis, including withholding treatment. The extent of the experiments was not fully known (and the experiments were not stopped) until the 1970s.

ACTIVITY 3.6

1. What are some other examples of historical events in the United States involving non-dominant groups that were underreported or misreported?

2. What are some examples of global events that have had a historical "shift" in thinking?

3. Why do inaccurate historical representations exist?

4. Who benefits from inaccurate historical representations?

5. Who is adversely affected by inaccurate historical representations?

Genuine historical revisionism is an accepted part of historical study. The examples of the "rewriting" of history given on the previous page represent corrections of fact or omission. In those examples, the inaccurate or omitted facts benefited dominant groups.

There are also examples of extensively documented historical events that are currently being questioned that do not reflect accurate historical revisionism. One of the most publicized recent examples is the movement of Neo-Nazi groups and Nazi sympathizers (both inside and outside of the United States) to discount the extent of or, in some cases, the existence of the Holocaust. The Holocaust denial movement is extremely painful for Jewish survivors in the United States and Europe, as well as others who believe that the lessons of the Holocaust must be remembered and used to interpret and respond to current and future examples of hatred. In 2000, for example, Austria received worldwide attention when a politician who often expressed support of Nazi principles, and who is strongly opposed to foreign immigration into Austria, was elected to a high-level governmental position.

Example: Holocaust Deniers

There are many examples of writers in the United States and Europe who have been called "Holocaust deniers"—people who question either the existence or extent of the Holocaust. David Irving is an English author who has written extensively about World War II and the Holocaust. He has expressed admiration for Hitler and German SS officers and has questioned the historical interpretation of the Holocaust. He spent several years living in Germany as a young adult. Although he has no academic training as a historian, he presents himself as a historian in his writing.

In 1999, David Irving filed libel charges in England against a history professor in the United States whose specialty area is in Holocaust studies. The professor included Irving in a discussion in her book about holocaust deniers. In 2000, the libel charges were found to be unfounded.

ACTIVITY 3.7

1. What is your initial reaction to the brief description of the incident described in the previous example?

2. Develop a list of questions about Holocaust denial.

3. Find answers to your questions in published accounts of the controversy. You can use the Internet to help identify perspectives. Note the perspective of each source.

4. Develop a list of perspectives and issues related to Holocaust denial.

5. Describe your opinion about Holocaust denial. How has your opinion changed or remained the same based on your exploration?

6. How does this example compare and contrast with other examples of shifts in historical perspective?

Art and Design

MUSEUM ISSUES IN ART AND DESIGN

Museums have increasingly explored the cultural aspects of display. For example, is it appropriate to display cultural artifacts designed for everyday use in a museum setting? Particularly in the case of death rituals and artifacts, issues of respect and cultural sensitivity are often discussed. While it is not unusual to see Native-American artifacts displayed in museum settings, digging up European-American graves to display bodies and burial elements is considered unthinkable.

Another diversity issue museums have faced is that of exhibits that may be offensive to some viewers. In the early 1990s, the photographic work of Robert Mapplethorpe received national attention because of the controversy generated by some photographs of homosexual men and naked children. In 1999, an exhibit at the Brooklyn Museum that had offensive religious overtones for some so outraged then-New York mayor Rudolf Giuliani that he threatened to cut funding for the museum.

ACTIVITY 3.8

1. What is your initial opinion of the Brooklyn Museum example?

2. What is your opinion about artistic expression in general?

3. List as many issues and values inherent in the Brooklyn Museum example as you can.

CURRICULAR ISSUES IN ART AND DESIGN

At the campus level, curricula in art history and design have often focused on European cultures. Requirements for art, architecture and interior design usually include survey courses on Western European art and design. Asian and African design have only recently been added to many college curricula and are often elective rather than required courses.

GENDER ISSUES IN ART AND DESIGN

In many disciplines, including art and design, there are status hierarchies that correspond to the gender domination of the field. For example, disciplines that are dominated by women, such as interior design and fiber arts, often have less status than their male-dominated counterparts, such as architecture.

ACTIVITY 3.9

1. How would it feel to have someone else's art always held up as the "classic?"

2. How does lack of awareness of some types of art and design create barriers to diversity understanding?

3. Why do you think male-dominated design disciplines often have more status than female-dominated disciplines?

Business

The increase in international and multinational corporations, as well as global businesses, has led to a focus on several issues in business curricula. Negotiation, team building, and cross-cultural communication are examples. There are many books that focus on preparing people for international business skills. When one is exploring differences in business practices, manners and communication styles, the emphasis is usually on increasing awareness as a way to avoid cultural mistakes that would have an adverse effect on the business.

There are many examples of ethical issues in business. The working conditions and pay of workers at foreign plants of United States companies, the environmental impact of the practices of United States companies around the world, and corporations defining the ethical social responsibility differently in different countries are just a few examples of ethical issues in business.

Activity 3.10

1. What are other examples of current events and issues that reflect ethical issues in business?

2. Select one example. What are the underlying assumptions and cultural values inherent in the example?

Science

Perhaps the least explored fields for diversity applications are in the physical sciences. Diversity connections often focus on gender (e.g., disproportionate number of male scientists). There are many other specific applications in various fields, particularly in the areas of values and ethics. Technology has created many new questions in medicine, genetic research and chemistry. Examples include cloning, gene therapy, infertility treatment and in vitro treatment of fetuses, among others. A recent controversy is related to the increased cost of testing to detect breast cancer because of a patent of the gene. Future technological advances will certainly result in even more issues that involve cultural values related to human life.

Activity 3.11

1. What are other examples of current events and issues that reflect ethical issues in science?

2. Select one example. What are the underlying assumptions and cultural values inherent in the example?

Education

Education, particularly in preparation for teaching in public schools, has many diversity connections. Some are philosophical, such as those inherent in defining the purpose of education or in identifying learning styles and types of intelligence. Others are specific to the demographics of the school, such as income, race and ethnicity of students. Others are part of content presentation in subject areas, such as the controversy over teaching evolution. Others are political, such as school funding strategies and use of vouchers.

One demographic shift that is already affecting schools is the changing demographics of Hispanics in the United States. A specific factor of interest is the number of second-generation Hispanics. Adults who immigrate to the United States (either illegally or legally) have children who are citizens by birth and are usually bilingual. According to FreeRepublic.com (self-defined as "A Conservative News Forum"), in 2000, first-generation Hispanic immigrants totaled 14.2 million, and children of immigrants totaled 9.9 million. Projections for 2020 are 20.6 million first generation and 21.7 second generation.

The increase in Hispanic students will be important in schools. Issues of assimilation, acculturation, and language, among others, will be important, but will also change over time to adapt to the impact of shifts in first-generation and second-generation students.

Example: School Vouchers

The issue of school vouchers is very complex and will be briefly described here to serve as a starting point for discussion. Basically, school vouchers enable parents to send their children to private schools by giving them a credit of a certain amount of money. Proponents of school vouchers say that children in failing public schools should not be forced to stay there, that vouchers "even the playing field" for people from different socioeconomic levels, and that the ability of children to leave public schools will provide incentive for public schools to do a better job.

Opponents of school vouchers say that the amount of credit is rarely enough to pay for the total cost of private schools (thus disadvantaging low-income students), that private schools cannot absorb large numbers of children with vouchers, and that challenges to public schools will not be addressed by voucher programs.

ACTIVITY 3.12

1. What is your initial opinion about school vouchers?

2. What other information do you need to know about the issue, and how would you find that information?

3. What are other diversity-related issues in education?

Your Major

Your major field of study might or might not have been included in the examples from this section. The examples can be used to help you identify the issues in your own field that will impact you in your professional career.

ACTIVITY 3.13

1. Identify five issues in your major field of study that have diversity connections.

2. Identify five diversity issues in your major that have interdisciplinary connections with other disciplines.

3. Identify five societal values and beliefs that are part of your major field of study.

ACTIVITY 3.14

1. List five current diversity-related issues in the news.

2. As a class group, list all the individually identified issues. Identify which are local (university/community), regional or state, national or international.

3. Discuss which issues are most relevant to you. Where on your diversity triangle are the issues you find most relevant?

4. How is an understanding of current events at different levels (e.g., individual, national, global) related?

Cultural Programming, Conflict and Conflict Resolution, and Use of Language

"You cannot shake hands with a clenched fist."

Indira Gandhi

Objectives of Chapter 4

The overall objective of Chapter 4 is to explore three important concepts in diversity: cultural programming, conflict and conflict resolution, and use of language. Chapter 4 expands on concepts introduced in previous chapters. Specific objectives of Chapter 4 follow.

❖ Understand sources of individual cultural programming
❖ Learn about the impact of personal choices in cultural programming
❖ Explore conflict and individual conflict resolution styles
❖ Identify barriers to understanding multiple perspectives of issues
❖ Practice articulating perspectives different from one's own
❖ Explore use of language as a way to enhance understanding of multiple perspectives

Introduction

As we have seen in the previous chapters, types of diversity are complex and interrelated. Individuals are also complex. Each person is a product of multiple influences.

This chapter focuses on the coupling of the complexity of diversity with the complexity of each individual person. Exploring sources of cultural programming and individual choices in cultural programming from a personal perspec- tive will enhance self-awareness, an important prerequisite to understanding others.

Sources of Cultural Programming

Each person has attitudes and beliefs about the types of diversity discussed in previous chap- ters. Cultural programming is the collective influences from life experiences that shape those attitudes and beliefs. Family, friends and many other people and activities influence our beliefs.

Activity 4.1

1. List five ways your family members have contributed to your values and beliefs.

2. List five ways your friends have contributed to your values and beliefs.

3. List five ways your university has contributed to your values and beliefs.

4. List five additional sources of cultural programming (e.g., religion, sports)

Personal Choices in Cultural Programming

Some of the sources of cultural program- ming that affect each of us are predetermined. For example, you do not have control over who your family is or where you are born. However, you choose or have control over many other sources of your cultural programming. The fol- lowing activity is designed to help you explore the choices you have made and can make in the future. The activity focuses on race and ethnic- ity. Additional parallel activities can be used for religion, gender, socio-economic status, disabil- ity and other forms of diversity.

Activity 4.2

Step One:

Use the following questions to fill out the table on the following page.

A. List five individuals or groups who are important to you.

B. List five service or professional people with whom you have contact (e.g., doctor, dentist, hair stylist).

C. List five people who represent your university in a significant way (e.g., university president, chair of the department in your major).

D. List five people (or groups) in the media you would consider your favorites (e.g., favorite movie actor/actress, favorite television actor/actress, favorite musician or musical group, favorite author).

Step Two:

Label each of the 20 individuals or groups by their race or ethnicity.

Using "C" to indicate "choice," and "N" to indicate "no choice," label each of the 20 individuals or groups by whether or not you have a choice about their inclusion in your list (e.g., dentist = C, parent = N)

Step Three:

1. What races or ethnicities are the majority of the people you listed?

2. Reflect on the meaning of your list. For example, what does it mean if your list includes mostly people of the same race or ethnicity? What does it mean if you have many different races or ethnicities?

3. In categories where you indicated you have a choice, why are your races and ethnicities the ones that they are?

4. How do the races and ethnicities reflect the demographics of your community, state, the country and the world?

5. In what ways are you satisfied with your list? In what ways are you dissatisfied? How could you change your list?

6. What are the implications for your ability to work in jobs and other environments having diverse demographics?

ACTIVITY **4.2**, CONTINUED

	Race	Choice/ No Choice
A. Individuals or groups		
1.		
2.		
3.		
4.		
5.		
B. Service or professional people		
1.		
2.		
3.		
4.		
5.		
C. Who represent your university in a significant way		
1.		
2.		
3.		
4.		
5.		
D. People (or groups) in the media you would consider your favorites		
1.		
2.		
3.		
4.		
5.		

Conflict and Individual Conflict Resolution Styles

Because individuals and cultures are complex, conflict is inevitable in interactions between people. Conflict can be defined as differences in values, opinions or ways of doing things. There are many conflict resolution styles, including competitiveness, cooperation, compromise, collaboration, consensus and avoidance. Communication patterns and the relationship of communication styles to conflict and conflict resolution strategies is the subject of study in many disciplines. Cross-cultural negotiation and international business practices are two examples of ways cultural communication patterns are explored.

The discussion in this section is limited to some basic assumptions about how communication styles relate to conflict and its resolution, and application of those assumptions to specific diversity-related and interpersonal examples. While the section is designed to help students begin to explore conflict in their own lives and interpret conflict in national and global situations, students are encouraged to explore the rich literature in communication, conflict and negotiation more deeply beyond the scope of this book. The following is a sample of individual and cultural assumptions related to conflict.

♦ Conflict resolution styles are situational. For example, the way you resolve conflict with family members may be very different from your style in a work setting.

♦ Your conflict style may vary depending on how salient the issue is to you. For example, you may be more competitive in a conflict about something important to you, and more willing to compromise about something less important to you.

♦ Conflict is often positive, creating opportunities for new solutions to challenges. This is in contrast to the assumption made by some people that conflict is negative and should be avoided.

♦ Self-awareness of your conflict resolution styles (and those of others) can help you work more effectively with people.

♦ Identifying conflict in early stages will improve the chances of resolution. For example, an initial disagreement between people who live together about how to extract toothpaste from a tube will more likely be resolved with an immediate discussion of toothpaste than if the disagreement is left unattended to become accusations of each other's character.

♦ There are often gender, ethnic or other diversity-related differences in conflict resolution style. However, within groups there is also individual variability.

ACTIVITY 4.3

1. In what types of situations are you more likely to be competitive in conflicts? What are the benefits and limitations of being competitive?

2. In what types of situations are you more likely to avoid conflict? What are the benefits and limitations of avoiding conflict?

3. In what types of situations are you more likely to look for compromise? What are the benefits and limitations of compromise?

4. In what types of situations are you more likely to look for consensus? What are the benefits and limitations of consensus?

Activity 4.4

1. Describe a situation where you experienced conflict that did not get resolved to your satisfaction.

2. Describe the conflict styles of the people involved.

3. Describe factors that led to the poor outcome of the situation (e.g., interaction of conflict styles, salience of the issue to one or more people).

4. If the situation were repeated, what could you do differently to ensure a more favorable outcome?

Activity 4.5

At a local hospital, two patients will be selected to receive two available donor livers. There are several people on the list of possible recipients. For the purpose of this exercise, assume that each person has an equal chance of survival and recovery if he or she receives a transplant. Because of the severity of their health conditions and the rarity of other acceptable organs for transplant, assume that the people who do not receive a liver transplant will certainly die.

In groups of 4 or 5 people, make a decision about which two people from the following list will get the two available livers. There are only two rules that must be followed. First, the group decision must be reached by consensus. Every group member must participate in the process, and all group members must agree on the two choices. Second, the group should not make assumptions about the liver transplant candidates that go beyond the information given. Remember, each person has an equal chance of survival and recovery if they receive a transplant. Complete the following steps.

1. As individuals, read through the list of candidates and make preliminary individual decisions about who should get the livers.
2. As a group, develop a decision-making process that will be used.
3. Follow the decision-making process. Take notes as the process occurs.
4. List the two candidates who will receive the liver transplant.
5. Give the rationale for your choices.
6. After completing steps 1 through 5, your instructor will give you additional information about each candidate.
7. Reevaluate your original choices. If your choices remain the same, discuss why. If your choices change, discuss why.

ACTIVITY 4.5, CONTINUED

Here is the information about each of the six potential transplant candidates.

a. Joe is a scientist who is close to finding a cure for AIDS. ~white supremicist~

b. Ramon is a college student. He plans to be a teacher. ~37 not citizen~

c. Emily is a mother of two young children. ~prostitute~

d. Olivia is a former illegal drug user who has been in recovery for the last 3 years. ~alcoholic~

e. Tyrone is a 47-year-old executive of a Fortune 500 company. ~pedophile~

f. Keisha works at a local fast food restaurant. ~18, scholarship to Harvard~

Discussion questions for the class:

1. Compare the processes used by each group to make decisions.

2. Discuss conflict within the groups and how conflict was resolved.

3. List the values that were part of the decision-making process.

4. How difficult was it to make decisions without making assumptions?

5. How difficult was it to reach consensus within the groups?

(Note to instructor: See Instructor's Guide.)

Understanding Multiple Perspectives

It is often difficult to hear perspectives that are different from our own. Particularly in areas where there are strong opinions, hearing another side or multiple perspectives may be interpreted as acceptance of something we do not believe. Apartheid, the "ethnic cleansing" of Bosnia, the Holocaust, genital mutilation, past and present slavery, and hate crimes are just a few examples of events and issues that do not and should not have to be considered acceptable. However, understanding is not synonymous with acceptance, and the value of understanding lies in the knowledge gained.

The inherent discomfort in listening to and trying to understand things that we do not agree with is often based on the erroneous assumption that values will be undermined with a greater understanding of multiple perspectives. That discomfort leads to the following.

◆ Culturally, we look at controversial issues as being two-sided, when in reality complex issues have multiple and complex perspectives.

◆ We are likely to accept one side as right and the other as wrong.

◆ We are more likely to hear things that are consistent with our belief system and ignore things that are not consistent with our belief system.

These three factors contribute (among others) to a lack of real understanding of multiple perspectives. Understanding multiple perspectives, whether we agree with them or not, is essential to understanding of diversity.

Example: Multiple Perspectives

In a senior interior design studio that I taught, we were doing a project incorporating the Chinese design principles of Feng Shui. A brief discussion of the importance of awareness and understanding of multicultural design perspectives was included in the introduction of the project.

One student appeared extremely uncomfortable with the project. Anticipating that it was related to workload or other aspects of the project requirements, I asked her if she had any questions. Her response was startling.

"I have friends in other majors who are always complaining that they are forced to hear about multiculturalism in their classes. They feel like diversity is being shoved down their throats. Whenever they have asked me if that is the case in interior design, I have always been able to say that it isn't. I have felt like interior design is a safe major—and now I know that it is not—diversity is being shoved down our throats here, too."

The initial response to the student's comments was stunned silence, followed by a number of students arguing the merits of multiculturalism and diversity. She was clearly outnumbered, and I sensed that the discussion could quickly turn into a majority-rules shouting match.

I asked the student to explain why she felt the way she did. After a series of questions and answers, it became clear that hers was a religious objection. She was very active in Campus Crusade for Christ, and planned to make a career doing missionary work converting people to Christianity. She felt that to accept the validity of other cultures (specifically in the context of religious beliefs) was to deny her own. As a future missionary, her perspective was that all people should be converted to the "truth." Religion as "value free" was not an option for her, and she perceived that the underlying assumptions in multiculturalism and diversity were a threat to her beliefs.

The discussion did not change opinions. It did, however, allow everyone the opportunity to better understand why the differences in opinion existed.

ACTIVITY 4.6

Use the preceding example to respond to the following.

1. What do you think influenced the students in the class to quickly label the student's opinion as wrong?

2. What values and beliefs contributed to each perspective?

3. Using an example from your personal experiences, describe how the barriers to understanding multiple perspectives impacted on your example.

4. How can you balance your own belief systems with those of others in a work or other setting?

Example: Vacation

A student saves money to go to a Mexican resort for a week. The resort is on the waterfront, so much of the time during the day is spent on the beach and in the hotel. Major activities during the evening are eating, drinking and dancing in the local bars and clubs. Most of the guests in the restaurants and clubs are also college students.

During a bus trip into the inland jungles, the student notices some houses near the road where the bus is passing. Huts made of bamboo and grass are grouped in clusters to form small villages. Small children and animals, including chickens and dogs, play near the streets in front of the dwellings. There are no doors on the houses—looking inside the student sees that there is no furniture on the floor of the dwelling.

ACTIVITY 4.7

1. What are your first impressions of the culture described in the preceding example?

2. Describe in as much detail as you can the characteristics of the culture.

3. Look over your answers to the two previous questions. What cultural assumptions are present?

4. How are those cultural assumptions related to stereotyping, ethnocentrism and understanding multiple perspectives?

5. How can the context of the interactions (e.g., vacationing, very limited exposure) create possibly erroneous cultural impressions?

(Note to instructor: See Instructor's Guide.)

The Importance of a Common Vocabulary and Use of Language in Exploring Diversity Issues

Understanding the power of language and words can be useful in understanding the complexities of diversity issues. The underlying meanings and derivations of words are powerful tools in communicating the reasons for use of words. Three dimensions will be explored in this section—language as a way to raise awareness of concepts, language as a way to facilitate informed discussion about controversial issues, and language use in dominant culture perspectives. Activity 4.8 is a pretest to measure knowledge of terms used to refer to groups of people.

Activity 4.8

Give your definitions for the following names that are used to represent groups of people:

	Definition	Synonyms?	Positive, Neutral or Negative?	If negative, why?
African American				
American Indian				
Native American				
Appalachian American				
Asian American				
European American				
Caucasian American				
Hispanic American				
Black				
White				
Chicano				
Chicana				
Latino				
Latina				
Oriental				

ACTIVITY **4.8**, CONTINUED

	Definition	Synonyms?	Positive, Neutral or Negative?	If negative, why?
Pacific Islander				
People of Color				
Homosexual				
Heterosexual				
Man				
Woman				
Elderly				
Jew				
Christian				
Muslim				
Hindu				
Buddhist				
Middle class				
Lower class				
Working class				
Upper class				
Person with a disability				
Handicapped				

LANGUAGE RAISES AWARENESS OF CONCEPTS

Sharing a common vocabulary and use of language can never be fully accomplished since we all see different things in our mind's eye based on our own experiences. Nevertheless, attempting a common vocabulary and use of language is an important prerequisite to awareness, understanding and application of diversity concepts for several reasons. First, language raises awareness of concepts, such as how cultural groups are defined. Names such as "Asian" or "Latino" group several cultures together. The term "Asian" includes people from many countries, including Cambodia, China, Japan, Korea, Thailand, and Vietnam. Similarly, the term "Latino/Latina" includes people from many countries and cultures, including Central America (e.g., El Salvador, Guatemala, Mexico, Nicaragua), South America, (e.g., Argentina, Brazil, Peru, Uruguay) and the Caribbean (e.g., Cuba, Dominican Republic, Puerto Rico). Obviously, the terms Asian and Latino/Latina are very broad, respectively representing countries with very different cultures from each other. "Native American Indian" is often used to refer to the hundreds of tribes and nations within the United States. Referring to someone by their specific tribal name (e.g., Lumbee, Ojibway, Miami tribe) is more accurate and respectful of the unique culture.

As often as possible it is helpful to consider each individual as a complex compilation of many cultures and types of diversity. In most cases, it is preferable to refer to a person as an individual person, rather than as a series of labels first. When cultural descriptors are necessary, it is best to refer to a person in the most specific cultural terms possible rather than by terms that group several cultures together. It is also more descriptive, accurate and respectful of cultural differences.

There are sometimes shifts in thinking about what groups are called. For example, the use of the term "colored" to refer to people of African descent was widely used in the United States until the late 1800s, followed by Negro until the 1960s. Reasons for the disuse of both terms (and many other terms now considered derogatory for racial and ethnic groups) are complex, and represent both historical and present-day dimensions. Similarly, there are preferences by individuals within groups for language generally considered acceptable. Examples include "Black" or "African American" and "Native American" or "American Indian" or "Native American Indian."

Two other examples of somewhat pejorative terms related to gender identity area "transvestite" and "hermaphrodite." A transvestite is a cross-dresser. Hermaphrodite refers to someone who is intersexual. Both preferred terms are more accurate and specific.

Sometimes, derogatory language is "taken back" by the group against which it is used. For example, "queer" was used as a slur against gays. Gays began using "Queer" to denote ownership of the term, as in "Queer Studies" for research. (Note that "Queer" is often capitalized when used in gay studies.)

The use of language to label by race or other types of diversity sometimes misrepresents dominant culture. For example, many "Afro Cubans" and other Blacks from Latin American countries identify more with the Hispanic cultures than Black cultures.

Although concepts of race and ethnicity are the most obvious examples of exploring language to raise awareness, other types of diversity can be examined as well. For example, language used to refer to people who are poor reflects a culture's attitudes. Terms such as "lower class" (implying a status hierarchy) and "White trash" (with elements of race, education and income) are a few examples.

Another subtle example relates to colleges and universities. Many universities have multiple campuses, usually within the same state. Sometimes there is one larger campus that is called the "main" campus. Smaller campuses within a university system are frequently called "branch" campuses. For the people on "branch" campuses the language may be problematic, particularly when the smaller campuses have their own programs, unique majors and autonomy from the larger campuses. The use of language that implies a campus is "lesser" can contribute to marginalization in other ways as well (e.g., stereotypes about faculty, students and educational programs). Although a specific system may have preferred language (e.g, regional campus, satellite campus), "branch" will be used in this book because it is the most commonly understood term throughout the U.S. "Branch" will be put in quotes to acknowledge the problematic nature of the term.

Another example of controversial language is the word "nondominant." In some cases, such as when a university requires students to take a course or courses representing nondominant perspectives, the word may have a subtle connotation of "lesser" attributed to cultures that are different. The differences in economics, use of technology, industrialization or other factors may be viewed from an ethnocentric perspective as undesirable, and the use of the term nondominant may contribute to that ethnocentrism.

"Nondominant" is appropriate when used in the context of exploring dominant privilege. It is that usage that is included in this book.

The Impact of Language: Distinguishing between Offensive and Hurtful Language

There is widespread acceptance of the offensive or hurtful nature of many words that are used in a derogatory way to describe race, ethnicity, gender, sexual orientation, religion, disability and other forms of diversity. However, there are many examples of words that are commonly used that are considered offensive or hurtful by many people.

The use of racially offensive or hurtful mascot names for sports teams is a highly visible example of language use. The Cleveland Indians and the Atlanta Braves are two examples. The term "Redskins" is also widely used in both professional and school sports. Some experts believe the derivation of the term "Redskins" dates to the United States practice of settlers selling American Indian scalps along with the pelts of bear, beaver, raccoon and other animals. Others believe the term was popularized in Western movies.

When trying to understand a perspective that may not seem important to you or that you disagree with, it is helpful to think about the distinction between what is offensive and what is hurtful. Often people who support the use of racial mascot names argue that anyone who is offended is simply being too sensitive. To say that someone is offended implies they have a choice to be offended or not to be offended; also, being offended often implies anger. Something that is hurtful to a person, on the other hand, is very personally felt. Most people do not intentionally try to hurt others, and viewing derogatory language as hurtful rather than offensive is a first step in understanding the impact of derogatory language on people.

Language Related to Culture Often Represents a Dominant Culture Perspective

Language is often descriptive in exploring dominant perspective views. "Dominant perspective" refers to the perspective that is held by the group that has the most power. In some cases, the power may be in numbers of people (e.g., majority of Whites in the United States).

Example: The Use of Racial Mascot Names

I was attending a local conference for K–12 and university teachers at a local suburban high school. It was clear that considerable attention had been paid to readying the building for the conference—signs were posted directing participants to activities, bulletin boards and display cases were showcasing the various activities of classes within the school, and staff were on hand to help out in many ways. As I walked down one major hallway toward a classroom where a number of conference sessions were held, there was a large banner, probably three or four feet high and 15 feet long, promoting an upcoming sports event. It read: "Scalp the Indians—go Mavericks."

In other cases, it may be in status or some other indicator of power (e.g., high proportion of male executives in business in the United States).

Language may be used to support a position or negate an opposing one. For example, in the war in Iraq, the war is referred to as the "war on terrorism." Soldiers in support of the United States are called "coalition forces" in the United States, and "occupiers" in Iraq. Such language is not unique historically or geographically. During what Northerners called the "Civil War," Southerners referred to the war as "the War for Southern Independence" and "the War of Northern Aggression." Those fighting in northern Ireland are called "freedom fighters" or "terrorists," depending on the perspective of the speaker.

ACTIVITY **4.9**

1. The banner described in the previous example sent what messages about the values and beliefs of the school culture?

2. What (if anything) should the participants in the conference have done?

3. Give examples of commonly used terms that could be considered derogatory by individuals or groups. Rephrase each term to apply to another group. How is the interpretation different if another group is used? (Example: Replace "Hooters" with a male body part. Replace "Redskin" with "paleface," "Whiteskin" or "Blackskin.")

4. In your list of examples of commonly used derogatory terms, what types of diversity are most often represented? Are there more slurs about age, sexual orientation, geographic location within the United States, etc.?

5. Put the individual lists together into a class list. What terms do you find most offensive? Analyze why some are more offensive to you than others.

6. Speculate about why some forms of diversity are more likely to have commonly used derogatory terms than other forms of diversity.

7. Discuss the perspectives (both pro and con) about using Indian names for sports mascots.

Example: Hurtful Language

A first-year student is walking across campus the first week of class. She loves the university, it is a beautiful day, and she is thinking how happy she is at the university and how friendly people are. As she passes a residence hall, a smiling male says "hi" from an upstairs window. As she smiles and waves back, thinking again how friendly everyone seems to be at the university, the male shouts out to the athletic, average-sized student "Why don't you go on a diet, you fat bitch." Several of his friends in the residence hall hear the comment, laugh and look out the window to see the young woman, who is devastated. During the next several weeks she contemplates leaving school.

ACTIVITY 4.10

Use the preceding example to respond to the following.

1. What would your reaction have been if this happened to you?

2. Think of an example of something related to your identity that you might be called that would be hurtful to you. Why would it be hurtful?

3. Why do you think the young woman reacted the way she did?

4. What do you think the male student intended in the comment?

ACTIVITY 4.11

A European-American staff member of the African-American mayor of Washington, D.C. used the word "niggardly" in a conversation with two of his co-workers. The word, which means "miserly" and has no racial derivation, was used in the context of a budget discussion. One of the co-workers was offended, and the situation quickly escalated into a perception that the staff member had used a racial slur. The staff member resigned from his position, but was eventually reinstated.

1. What is your initial reaction to the description of the incident?

2. Develop a list of questions about the incident.

3. Find answers to your questions in published accounts of the controversy.

4. Develop a list of perspectives and issues related to the incident.

5. Describe your opinion about the incident. How has your opinion changed or remained the same based on your exploration?

ACTIVITY 4.12

1. Make a list of five statements that are commonly used that might be offensive or hurtful. An example might be a male saying to someone in a softball game "You are throwing the ball like a girl" or "You are throwing the ball like a fag."

2. For each statement, list who might be offended.

3. For each statement, list who might be hurt.

4. Can you think of a time when you told or overheard a joke or a comment, not realizing that someone was there who might be hurt or offended?

5. Is it acceptable to tell a joke or make a comment about race, ethnicity, religion or gender if there is no one from the group present? Why or why not?

Although dominance is often related to majority, that is not always the case. In the United States and many other parts of the world, men and women have relatively equal numbers, but unequal dominance in society. Language often reflects cultural views on gender. For example, there are many negative terms for a woman who is sexually active with multiple partners, but few for men because of a double standard about sexual behavior. Descriptions of "success" for men and women are also often very different.

Two things should be noted about dominant perspective. First, individuals within the dominant groups do not always experience privilege. For example, although White males as a group are more likely to have higher paying jobs than female counterparts or males of color, an individual White male might not. It is analogous to actuarial tables used by insurance companies that statistically group people by age and health factors to determine average life expectancy. The tables do not predict when a specific individual will die.

Second, dominant perspective is relative. For example, the percentage of Asians and Asian Americans in the United States is relatively small. In the world, however, Asians represent a large percentage of the world population.

There are also geographic examples of dominant privilege. "America" often is used to refer to the United States. However, there are many countries in North, Central and South America that also consider themselves "Americas." "Nation" is often used to refer to the United States; yet there are 560 indigenous groups, including many nations. The use of the terms "Oriental" and "Third World" have their roots in political colonialism and domination. "The Orient" is often used interchangeably with "the East," suggesting a fixed reference point of "the West," which usually refers to Western Europe. Therefore, it represents a Eurocentric perspective.

Another example is in the use of the term "minority." Minority refers to groups that represent a smaller percentage of the total population of a larger group. Sometimes the term minority is erroneously used to refer to non-dominant groups who actually represent the majority in numbers. The following example illustrates the point.

There is disagreement regarding the hyphenation of "African American." The term "African American" (as opposed to "African-American" with a hyphen) is generally preferred. "Dropping the hyphen not only leads to a cleaner typographical look but may also help to cancel the connotation of marginality that comes with hyphenation." (Source: Philip Herbst, *The Color of Words: An Encyclopaedic Dictionary of Ethnic Bias in the United States*) You will notice throughout this book that African American is not hyphenated unless it is used as a compound modifier, thus following the rules of punctuation.

There are many examples of evolution of word usage for nondominant groups, including those that have been described earlier in this section. Another example emerged in the disability rights movement. Phrases like "crippled person" and "handicapped person" have been replaced with "person with a disability" or "person who is differently abled." There are at least two key reasons for the shift. First, language that puts the person first and the disability second more accurately reflects the whole person—someone who is a person with a disability instead of a disability with a person. Second, in most physical disabilities, it is the physical environment and the attitudes of others that create the negative effects of the disability, not the person who has a disability.

Person-first language has been adapted to other types of diversity as well. "People of color," although controversial for a variety of reasons, is an example of person-first language.

Example: Dominant Culture Language

During a session of a large national diversity conference, a European-American administrator at a large city college was talking about his institution. He used the term "minority" several times in reference to the predominantly African-American neighborhood and student body of the college. Unlike the administrator who was speaking, the majority of the session participants were African American. Every time the speaker used the term "minority" to refer to dominant African-American populations, other audience members looked at each other with amusement or disbelief. Finally, someone politely pointed out to him that in the context of his comments he was in the minority, not the African Americans he was discussing.

ACTIVITY 4.13

1. What are examples of non-person-first language you have heard in recent conversations or news events?

2. In the examples you have listed, how is the person potentially disadvantaged by the language use?

PART II

Understanding

Conceptual Framework to Explore Diversity Understanding: Characteristics of Culture

"If you don't crack the shell, you can't eat the nut."

Persian proverb

"The evil that is in the world almost always comes from ignorance, and good intentions may do as much harm as malevolence if they lack understanding."

Albert Camus, *The Plague*, 1947

Objectives of Chapter 5

The overall objective of Chapter 5 is to introduce conceptual frameworks for studying culture and to identify and explore examples of characteristics of culture that influence cultural patterns and behaviors. Specific objectives follow.

❖ Describe conceptual frameworks for studying culture
❖ Explore how components of culture (characteristics and systems) can be used to help understand cultures as a whole
❖ Examine the role of spatial concepts such as personal space, territoriality and privacy in cultures
❖ Identify relationships between leisure activities and cultural characteristics
❖ Examine the role of communication patterns in cultures
❖ Explore the concept of time in cultures
❖ Examine the derivation and impact of food and eating patterns in cultures
❖ Explore holiday rituals and activities in cultures
❖ Explore dress and appearance in culture

Conceptual Frameworks for Studying Culture

There are many conceptual frameworks that can be used to study culture and diversity concepts. Sleeter and Grant (1987) examine multicultural literature to identify five approaches used in multicultural education (see "An Analysis of Multicultural Education in the United States" in the *Harvard Educational Review*, Volume 57, Number 4, pages 421–444). One approach ("teaching the culturally different") educates students of color and other non-dominant groups about the dominant culture. A second approach ("human relations") teaches how diverse people can get along with each other. A third approach ("single group studies") focuses on the study of individual groups. A fourth approach ("multicultural education") stresses value and respect for diversity. A fifth approach ("education that is multicultural and social reconstructionist") expands on the "multicultural education" approach by stressing the importance of understanding the reasons for differences.

One way to explore cultures that integrates elements of several cultural approaches is to look at the characteristics and systems that make up a culture. Looking at components of culture individually and then as a whole is helpful in deconstructing complex ideas and relationships. By exploring the characteristics and systems of a culture or event, the complexity of culture can be more fully examined. Deconstructing differences between individuals or groups can also reduce stereotypes. This leads to a greater understanding of the "why" of difference and makes it easier to see both similarities and differences in cultures.

Characteristics and Systems of Culture

Characteristics of culture include the more individual components of culture, such as leisure activities, how people use physical space, communication patterns, time, food and eating patterns, clothing and dress, and holiday customs. Within a culture, there may be considerable similarity or variability in characteristics. There is a great deal of variability in the United States in characteristics of culture as well as systems of culture.

Systems of culture are the large institutional components of a culture, such as education, politics, economics, family and kinship patterns and religion. In multicultural settings such as the United States, descriptions of each system may be more complex than in other cultures because of the enormous variability in each system, and in the multiple cultural perspectives of people in the United States. Cultures also include shared values, norms, beliefs and ways of doing things and seeing the world.

It is often easier for a person to describe characteristics of culture than systems of culture, because characteristics are personally experienced and systems may be more abstract. However, our own personal and cultural attributes are so normative to us that they are often invisible. Also, it is likely in many cases that characteristics of culture are influenced by the larger systems of culture.

The characteristics and systems of culture framework can be applied to the analysis of any study of difference. The framework can be used to explore differences in types of diversity (e.g., race, ethnicity, gender, sexual orientation). It can also be used to explore differences at any level (e.g., local, national, global).

Introduction to Characteristics of Culture

Characteristics of culture are individual behaviors that reflect cultural values. When exploring the reasons for behaviors, characteristics of culture can provide a useful framework.

The concepts of characteristics of culture are important to cultural understanding for several reasons. First, there are many individual and cultural variations around the world. Second, the concepts are often unconscious and deeply ingrained in culture. The existence and meaning of differences are often misinterpreted, leading to misunderstanding or conflict. Third,

ACTIVITY 5.1

1. Pair up with a student in the class whom you do not know well.

2. Face each other and stand a comfortable distance apart.

3. Move toward each other until you begin to feel uncomfortable.

4. Look directly at your partner. Do not talk to each other, laugh or look away.

5. Hold the position until the instructor says to stop.

DISCUSSION QUESTIONS:

1. How did it feel to be "too close"?

2. What did you do to reduce discomfort?

3. How would you adapt if you knew your partner had different personal space boundaries?

4. Give an example of when you have experienced a personal space violation. How did it feel? What did you do?

even a conscious awareness of differences does not necessarily lead to the ability to culturally adapt in these areas.

There are many characteristics of culture. This chapter will focus on several, including personal space, territoriality and privacy; communication patterns; time orientations; leisure activities; food and eating patterns; holiday rituals and activities; and dress and appearance. Other characteristics may be apparent or dominant in some cultures. The characteristics selected for discussion are important in most cultures.

Personal Space, Territoriality and Privacy

Spatial concepts including personal space, territoriality and privacy are so central to cultural awareness and understanding that many anthropologists and other social scientists have studied them. In the seminal book *The Hidden Dimension*, Edward Hall coined the term "proxemics" to refer to the cultural use of space.

PERSONAL SPACE

Personal space is the invisible space around a person that is the person's comfort zone. Your personal space is portable—it goes where you go. Although sometimes referred to as a personal space bubble, the space is not circular. More space is required in front of the person than behind, and more space is required above the waist than below the waist.

The amount of personal space needed is individually and culturally variable. The personal space guidelines established by anthropologist Hall are the most common norms in the

United States. Hall describes four "zones" of territory. The zones range from comfortable distances required for close friends and families to distances required for strangers.

In other countries, there are different distances in personal space zones. For example, in some countries, what people in the United States would consider "normal" conversational distance would be considered to be too far away and therefore disrespectful.

In addition to individual and cultural variability, personal space needs are contextual. For example, what is comfortable in a public place during the day may be "too close" on a deserted street late at night.

An important point in understanding the impact of personal space is to know that even if you are aware of differences and that they are cultural, it is still uncomfortable to adapt to a cultural pattern that is very dissimilar to your own. The preceding activity probably illustrated that point. Given that, it is easier to understand how misunderstandings can easily be developed in situations where people have different cultural uses of space.

Example: Personal Space

In Malta, many of the buses are recycled from England. The English buses reflect the cool English climate, and often have thick fabric upholstery on the seats and windows that do not open. In the warm climate of Malta, the buses often are hot and stuffy. On one visit to Malta during summer, the high tourist season, I was riding a bus across the island. At first the bus was nearly empty, but soon it was extremely full, with all seats filled and many people standing in the aisle.

I was in the second set of seats back from the driver. In the front seat ahead of me, there was a young Maltese woman. Many of the passengers on the bus were tourists or casually dressed Maltese people, probably headed for the beach. The young woman was in business dress, and appeared somewhat uncomfortable with the increasing crowding on the bus.

The driver stopped to pick up one last passenger. The passenger was a Maltese man who stood in the aisle directly behind the driver. His back was facing the young Maltese woman, but his body was only about a foot from her. Neither person was able to increase the distance between them. She was seated. He was unable to move because of the number of other people in the aisle. Every time the bus hit a bump, the man moved slightly toward the young woman, who became increasingly uncomfortable. She stared at the man, even though he could not see her. Her body posture became stiff and tense. With each bump, he moved a bit closer. Her hands clenched, and I noticed her long red fingernails. The bus hit another bump, and her hand went to his back, scratching down its length. The man turned to look at the woman. Embarrassed and confused, he exited the bus at the next stop.

ACTIVITY 5.2

1. Do you consider the response of the young woman to be extreme? If so, what could she have done instead?

2. Think of an example of when your personal space was violated. How did you feel? What were your options for response? What did you do to reduce your discomfort?

TERRITORY

Territory differs from personal space in that there are often visible spatial cues. For example, territory may be "marked" by walls, fences, doors or the use of personal possessions. The amount of territory needed may be based on personal space needs or other factors.

There are several types of territory. Fixed territory is considered to be your territory whether you are using it or not. For example, in most parts of the United States you do not expect that people will enter and use your home when you are not there. An exception is in some parts of Northern Alaska, where for survival reasons it is illegal to lock the doors of homes in case someone is in need of shelter from the extreme winter temperatures.

Variable territory is territory that is yours only when you are using it. Examples of variable territory include phone booths and a specific class during a specific class time. Territory can also be situational—different in the same space at different points in time. For example, a college business and entertainment district may have different territorial norms during business hours than at night.

ACTIVITY 5.3

1. Give an example of when you have experienced a territory violation. How did it feel? What did you do?

2. How do you designate your territory in the following places?

   a. a shared living room

   b. your spot at a table in the library

   c. your seat on an airplane

   d. your position at a party in a friend's home

   e. a shared space in a residence hall (if applicable to you)

3. What are some examples of fixed, variable and situational territory?

ACTIVITY 5.4

(Adapted from a cross-cultural example given by Edward Hall in *The Hidden Dimension*.)

As a class, you are a cross-cultural negotiation team. You have been hired to negotiate a conflict situation between German and American executives in a German-based American company. During your initial meetings with the two groups, it is clear that the conflict has escalated to a point that affects the success of the company.

Each person on the team will ask the instructor a yes-no question about the situation. Each student should keep notes about the questions and answers.

After each student has asked a question, the class will divide into teams of three or four students to develop theories about the source of the conflict. The theories (and the rationale for each) will be presented to the class.

The instructor will tell the students the source of the conflict.

DISCUSSION:

1. Identify categories of questions that were asked.

2. What were the stereotypes and cultural assumptions built into the questions or speculations?

3. How were the answers to the questions used to develop theories about the source of the conflict?

4. What is the importance of awareness in this example?

5. Describe other examples where lack of awareness could lead to serious misunderstanding.

(Note to instructor: See Instructor's Guide.)

Examining cultural values and practices about neighborhoods where people live is a useful way to explore the meaning of personal space, territory and privacy. What kinds of residences are desired (e.g., detached houses, attached houses, apartments), how we arrange living spaces, and indoor-outdoor relationships are just a few examples of spatial concepts that reflect culture.

Example: Territory

Michael, a British student, arrives in the United States for his graduate work. His home in England is in a small and picturesque village located in the Midlands region of the country. It is the type of village found on picture post cards, with thatched roof houses, small fenced yards and roses climbing the fences. In the United States, he will be staying with a family in an upper income suburb of a large city.

A few months after arriving in the United States, Michael moves into a graduate dormitory at the University. He is asked to describe his experience in the United States so far. He responds that his first experience with the family in the suburbs led him to believe that people in the United States are cold, distant and unfriendly.

ACTIVITY 5.5

1. What physical differences between his homes in England and the United States may have given Michael his impressions about people in the United States?

2. Select an example of when you were in an unfamiliar environment. Describe the characteristics of the physical space.

3. How was the physical environment different from your most familiar environments?

4. In what ways could the physical environment have influenced your feelings about your interactions or impressions?

(Note to instructor: See Instructor's Guide.)

PRIVACY

As early as two years of age, my daughter Brenna could articulate a need for privacy. For her, ceremoniously marching into her bedroom and loudly shutting the door usually followed "I need privacy!" Equating privacy with physical distance and separation is not universal. On the contrary, the deeply ingrained connection in the United States between space and privacy is unusual. Three examples of alternate ways of achieving privacy follow.

Examples: Achieving Privacy

Example #1

The parents of a four-year-old Maltese child speak English in the home. When they want privacy in their conversation, they speak to each other in Maltese. However, they quickly realize that their son understands Maltese. They switch to Italian for private conversations. Since all Maltese television is broadcast from Italy in Italian, the parents soon learn that their son knows Italian. They begin to speak in French, but within a few months their son again understands what they are saying. The parents lament that they are out of shared languages, although the father speaks some Swedish and the mother speaks some German. They complain that they can no longer have private conversations.

Example #2

In an African village, the young unmarried men sleep in a large circular hut. Cots are located along the perimeter of the room and the center of the room is open and unfurnished. When an anthropologist asks a young man how privacy is achieved in the shared sleeping quarters, the young man seems perplexed by the question. After some discussion about the meaning of privacy, he responds that when he wants interaction with others, he faces toward the center of the room. When he does not want interaction, he faces toward the wall.

Example #3

In crowded cities around the world, people using subway systems often avert their eyes and avoid visual contact with other passengers. In Japan, it is also not uncommon for people to wear masks when they are ill in a polite attempt to protect others from common communicable diseases.

Kissing in France

ACTIVITY 5.6

1. Think about a time when you felt crowded. What did you do to reduce your discomfort?

2. What are other ways you have used to get privacy in crowded situations?

3. How would you describe the level of privacy you prefer?

4. In what ways have you seen differences in privacy (in traveling, observing people, etc.)?

5. Speculate about the reasons for the differences you have seen.

Communication

Communication encompasses many elements that relate to culture. The discussion in this section will include three of those elements—nonverbal communication, high- and low-context communication styles and regional dialects.

NONVERBAL COMMUNICATION

As discussed in the previous section, nonverbal communication is often used to establish or maintain personal space, territory or privacy. Body language, eye contact, facial expressions, hand shaking, hugging and kissing as a form of greeting are all examples of nonverbal communication techniques that can be culturally variable.

Because of the cultural variability of nonverbal communication, there is great potential for misreading nonverbal cues and misinterpreting the meaning. For example, a child looking down at a desk in a classroom might be labeled as inattentive, when in reality in the child's culture averting one's eyes is a sign of respect for authority.

Nonverbal communication can be an enhancement of or supplement to verbal communication or the whole form of communication. For example, nonverbal communication may be used exclusively by some people who are deaf, autistic, or have cerebral palsy, among other physical reasons.

HIGH-CONTEXT AND LOW-CONTEXT COMMUNICATION STYLES

Anthropologist Edward Hall is credited with identifying the concepts of high- and low-context communication. Context includes nonverbal and subtle communication cues from the person and the environment. Knowing whether a person or culture is high- or low-context in communication style is critical in the success of communication between people and cultures.

In high-context communication, verbal communication is often indirect and establishing the context of the communication is very important. The context may include making people feel comfortable through casual conversation, extensive interpretation of nonverbal behaviors and by attention to detail in the physical surroundings. An example of a high-context culture is Japan. (Recently, a man in Japan was charged and taken to court for not adequately greeting a coworker upon arriving at work in the morning.)

The use of American Sign Language (ASL) in Deaf culture also represents a high-context form of communication. It should be noted that ASL use in Deaf culture also has variations by other cultural characteristics beyond hearing. For example, a recent discussion on the National Public Radio Tavis Smiley Show indicated the need for more African-American sign language interpreters.

Low-context communication patterns are common in the United States. In low-context communication, verbal language is very important. What is explicitly said is most important and directness is often a valued part of the communication.

ACTIVITY 5.7

1. Do you consider yourself to be primarily high or low context in your communication style?

2. In what situations are you high context?

3. In what situations are you low context?

4. Describe how the following would be interpreted by someone from a high-context or a low-context culture:

   a. A business meeting that begins with "Let's start with agenda item one."

   b. A business meeting that begins with a lengthy discussion of the children of the attendees.

5. With which of the two scenarios in the previous question would you be most comfortable?

6. Describe how low-context communication would be defined by a high-context person.

7. Describe how high-context communication would be defined by a low-context person.

REGIONAL DIALECTS

Regional dialects are an example of a diversity issue related to standard language. Regional dialects in the United States (as well as accents from other countries) are often related to stereotypes about people from the region. Dialects include pronunciation of words, timing of speaking, use of grammar and phrases. For example, in some Southern states it is common to say "honey" or "dear" at the beginning of a conversation. The perception of the speaker is that leaving out those words would be abrupt and clipped, and therefore disrespectful. The perception of someone not used to the dialect might be the opposite—that being called "honey" or "dear" is itself a sign of disrespect.

As briefly discussed in Chapter 1, regional dialects can have either positive or negative stereotypes. Coupled with high- or low-context communication styles, there are endless combinations of communication patterns and consequent numerous possibilities for cultural misinterpretation and misunderstanding.

ACTIVITY 5.8

1. Do you think you have an accent? If so, what are the stereotypes of the accent? Have you experienced being stereotyped because of your accent? Describe an example. How did being stereotyped make you feel?

2. Describe several regional dialects and the stereotypes associated with them.

3. How do stereotypes about dialects cause bias? How could this be problematic?

4. What are other issues of language use in the United States (e.g., Ebonics, English-only policies, American Sign Language)?

5. List as many perspectives as possible for each issue identified in the previous question. For each, consider what is helpful and what is limiting about establishing a "standard" language in the United States.

Time

How time is viewed culturally relates to many things. In this section, three aspects of time will be included: (a) clock-time versus process-time, (b) time as an element of historical context and (c) cultural views on aging.

CLOCK-TIME AND PROCESS-TIME

Time orientation can vary from individual to individual and from culture to culture. Clock-time orientation places a value on punctuality and "efficiency" in the use of time as measured in minutes and hours. Not surprisingly, a clock-time orientation is often associated with values such as "getting to the point."

Process-time orientation places a value on the process of an activity rather than the clock time involved. In process-time orientation, the successful completion of a task or activity is an important factor, no matter how long it takes. Part of what determines success in process-time orientation may be relational-oriented—how people felt about the process and outcome may be very important.

Native American Indians and Latinos(as) often use process-time orientation. The time orientation is based on the belief that people will gather when everyone is ready and when they have completed other relational obligations that are also untimed and important. Since this is understood, no one is offended because it is assumed a person needed to be where he or she was at the time.

Example: Process-Time Orientation

My students were invited to an Ojibwe Indian pipe-smoking ceremony that was scheduled to occur during the normal class time. Most of the students were in their seats in the audience at the scheduled start time, but there were few others in the room. Slowly, people began to appear. After 15 minutes, none of the panel of tribe leaders had arrived. My students began to show signs of confusion and discomfort. They looked at their watches, each other and me. I purposefully sat quietly and did not respond. Then the leaders arrived. They quietly sat in their seats at the front of the room, looking down. Again, my students were uncomfortable. After another 10 minutes or so, one of the leaders began to speak, and the ceremony began. The ceremony ended when the leaders considered it to be complete. The end point was not dependent on the designated clock time for the end of the class.

ACTIVITY 5.9

1. What is the time orientation you are most comfortable using?

2. What are the benefits of your preferred time orientation?

3. What are the limitations of your preferred time orientation?

4. How often do you take longer than you intended to finish a process or complete a conversation? How do you feel about that when it happens?

5. Describe situations where you are always (or almost always) prompt.

6. Describe situations where you are always (or almost always) late.

7. Think about the time orientation of your culture at the university. During a normal day, what are some examples of where time orientation is important? How might a dominant time orientation affect the life of someone with a different time orientation?

8. Give examples of interpersonal conflict you have experienced or observed based on time orientation.

9. Discuss the relationship between time orientation and high- and low-context communication styles.

10. What are implications of time orientation for business practices?

11. What kinds of cultural values are communicated through the use of time?

TIME AS AN ELEMENT OF HISTORICAL CONTEXT

The importance of history in a culture is often reflected in the values of that culture. The age of the culture, physical manifestations of the past or many other factors may determine the level of importance. Level of importance of history may also impact perceptions of the present and the future.

The value of historical context can be used to explore diversity. Although in the United States there are shared celebrations and positive reminders of tradition and past events, there are also differences in interpretations of historical context. For example, in the United States, African Americans often stress the importance of the historical context of slavery and its implications for the experience of present-day African Americans. On the other hand, many descendants of early European Americans have a more present-oriented value that discounts the historical context, often arguing that "the

---

Examples: Historical Context Through Physical Surroundings

Example #1

In many villages and towns in England, bombed churches from World War II remain. The purpose of leaving the ruins is to remind people of the devastation of war. In one town, the church is located at the center of the main "roundabout"—a circular roadway that provides access to a number of major routes in the town. The roundabout is probably the busiest vehicular location in the city. Most people who drive see the church ruins every day and are reminded of the effects of war, in hopes of preventing another one.

Example #2

In Malta, just inside the main gate of the walled capital city of Valletta, there are ruins from an opulent opera house built in the late 1800s and destroyed in the 1940s during World War II. During the war, Malta was intensely bombed by Italy for two years. Many Maltese died, and many others starved or nearly starved when Malta was cut off from Allied supply ships for several years.

During a visit to Malta, I spent an afternoon at the ruins. Merchants used corners of the ruins as makeshift shops, and there were many large architectural elements, including columns and elegant limestone stairs, still intact. Upon returning to my flat, I told my neighbor about my day. She was Maltese, and had married a British soldier during the war. They had recently retired to Malta after spending several decades in England. She said "Oh, yes. The Royal Opera House. I remember we were there attending a symphony performance during our honeymoon. There was an air raid, so we went to the shelter. When we came out of the shelter, the Royal Opera House was gone."

The ruins of the Royal Opera House are controversial. Some people feel the ruins are an important reminder of the devastating effects of the war and should remain. Others feel that their presence is a deterrent to healing in the European community.

Example #3

In spring 2001 the Taliban planned to destroy all statues in Afghanistan. Many of the statues had significant artistic, historic, religious and cultural value. The international art community intervened to try to stop the destruction. Most if not all of the statues were destroyed.

past is the past," or "I am not responsible for what my ancestors did."

Another example is in religion. Although historical context is part of the structure of most religions, it is more explicit and important in some. Jews, for example, often integrate race, ethnicity and religion into being Jewish, in part because of the historical context of oppression experienced by Jewish people.

Physical manifestations often offer clues to the past. Effigies of ancestors provide a face to a distant past in churches. Styles of architecture suggest the values of the culture. For example, after the depression of the late 1920s and 1930s in the United States, most banks were built using design elements of ancient Greece, such as columns and pediments. This type of design was not an accident. Rather, it purposefully suggested stability, integrity, trustworthiness and other values banks were struggling to recapture in public perception.

Example: Historical Context

A Protestant woman of Scotch-Irish, English and German descent hired a Sephardic Jewish man from New York. As they became friends they frequently discussed their ancestry and religions. One day the woman said, "This may sound odd, but I just want to say how sorry I am about the Holocaust. Not all Germans are bad, you know." The man was quite touched and said, "I appreciate that. Wallowing in cultural guilt doesn't accomplish anything, but it's nice to hear a personal apology."

ACTIVITY 5.10

1. Think about where you grew up. What were examples of historical context through physical space? How well do you feel your culture was reflected?

2. What physical manifestations of cultural history are present at your university? List several and describe the historical message and cultural values that each gives.

3. How are the values identified in the previous question similar to your values? How are they dissimilar?

4. How important or unimportant do you think studying the history of the United States is in exploring issues of diversity?

5. What are some diversity examples of differences in perception of historical context that impede understanding of national or global diversity-related issues?

CULTURAL VIEWS ON AGING

The value placed on the elderly in a culture is a third way to explore the meaning of time in a culture. Whether those who have lived greater lengths of time are viewed as the carriers of wisdom or as being used up and worthless often reflect the value of time and historical context. The role of grandparents in families is an example of how cultural views on aging may vary. In some families, grandparents play an important role in socializing children and sharing family stories and histories. In other families, even when grandparents are nearby there is limited involvement.

ACTIVITY 5.11

1. What are the cultural advantages of being the age you are now?

2. What are the cultural disadvantages of being the age you are now?

3. Using the following words, describe the ages for each word when you think people are at their "most . . ."):

   a. productive

   b. beautiful

   c. strong

   d. wise

   e. happy

   f. powerful

   g. sexual

4. What do the answers in the previous question tell you about your cultural views on age?

5. In your opinion, what are cultural values related to age in the United States?

6. Give examples to support your answer in the previous question.

7. What are the benefits and limitations of a culture that values youth over higher ages?

8. What are the benefits and limitations of a culture that values higher ages over youth?

Leisure

Leisure activities, including hobbies and daily patterns, are both individually and culturally variable. Leisure activities are often related to systems of culture. For example, the leisure activities of a high school or college student may be tied directly to the campus activities of the educational institution. Someone who is very active in a church, synagogue or mosque may have leisure activities that are primarily related to his or her religion.

Choices in how leisure time is spent may be related to types of diversity, such as age, gender or socioeconomic status. For example, people who are involved in extreme sports are more likely to be young. Preferred leisure activities of men and women vary by gender, although an individual man or woman may differ from the stereotypical pattern. Socioeconomic status will likely affect access to activities in country clubs and ice rinks, for example.

Available and popular leisure activities are often regional and based in part on climate and geography. The afternoon siesta often found in countries with hot climates reflects the pre-air conditioning practicality of limiting activity during the hottest part of the day and working more in the early morning and in the evening. Coastal activities in the cooler northern parts of the United States, including New England, Washington and Oregon, differ from the warmer southern states, such as Florida and California.

Example: Leisure

In Duluth, Minnesota, the winters are long and cold. Although it is unclear whether it is true, locals proudly credit Mark Twain with saying, "The coldest winter I ever spent was the summer I spent in Duluth." Since the temperature of Lake Superior remains cool throughout the summer due to its large size, Duluth enjoys a "lake effect" in the summer months—a natural form of air conditioning that produces warm days and cool nights. Summer months are July and August; temperatures in the 40s and 50s (degrees Fahrenheit) in June are not uncommon, with many rainy days. There is usually some snow during October, with snowfall that stays on the ground beginning in November. March and even April snowfalls are not uncommon. The ice on Lake Superior is usually completely melted in April. I remember sitting in a restaurant with a group of friends in mid-March. We were looking out at the ice-covered Lake Superior. One of my normally reserved friends became excited and exclaimed in all seriousness, "Look, there's an ice breaker coming through! It's spring!"

Predictably, winter leisure activities such as cross-country and downhill skiing, snowmobiling, snowshoeing, ice fishing and winter camping are popular in northern Minnesota. People who are involved in active winter sports can describe snow and weather conditions in great detail. There are many more winter and snow words, illustrating the effect of culture on language. Stereotypes and competing use of land between cross-country skiers, downhill skiers and snowmobilers create conflicts unique to cold winter climate cultures.

ACTIVITY 5.12

1. What are your most common leisure activities?

2. What aspects of your culture influence your choice of leisure activities?

3. What are the dominant leisure activities in your college?

4. How do climate and geography affect your leisure activities?

5. Who might not have access to your preferred leisure activities?

Food and Eating Patterns

Food and eating patterns reflect many aspects of culture and are highly interrelated to characteristics and systems. For example, in the United States, the explosion in the number of fast-food restaurants and convenience foods available at supermarkets reflects changing lifestyles and attitudes about food preparation. People are spending more time at work outside of the home and there are more dual-career couples than in previous generations. Preparing food from "scratch" is often limited to holiday meals and special occasions. Technological advances such as refrigeration and microwave ovens have dramatically changed food preparation.

Example: American Paradigms in the United States

I attended a 12-day conference in New Hampshire with 20 other participants from the United States, Canada and England. The conference was at a remote conference center, and there was no opportunity for travel or exploration of the surrounding areas, much to the disappointment of all of us, especially the international participants. One person, an engineer from England, was to be joined by his wife and children at the end of the conference for a two-week holiday in the United States. On the last day of the conference, the meetings ended at noon. I had a car, and I asked the engineer if he wanted to join me in an afternoon of sightseeing. He accepted my invitation. As we were driving, I asked him if there was anything special he wanted to see or do in anticipation of his family's arrival. He responded that the one thing he wanted to do was to go through a "drive-thru" restaurant. He explained that there were no drive-thrus in his city in England, and that he had no idea how they operated. He wanted to practice the process before picking up his rental car and his family. I agreed, and he intently watched the process of ordering and receiving soft drinks.

The types of available foods in an area often greatly influence regional characteristics. Rice as a staple in many Asian countries reflects the ease of growing rice and the scarcity of other food items, such as meat. Fish in coastal area, scones and clotted cream (available because of the significant presence of dairy cows) in southwestern England, and potatoes in Ireland are a few examples of food preferences based on availability of ingredients. Beef and pork, readily available in the United States, are very resource-intensive to produce, requiring significant land (for feed crop production) that is not available in much of the world. The importation of fruits and vegetables has altered the need for seasonal adaptations in food choices by making some foods available year round.

Example: American Paradigms in Europe

During my first trip outside of the United States, I arrived at my residence hall at the University of Birmingham in England tired and thirsty. The trip had been about 24 hours from destination to destination, and there were meetings scheduled a few hours after my arrival in Birmingham. I found the vending machines, hoping for a carbonated drink with caffeine. Not finding any familiar colas, I selected an unfamiliar brand called Shandy. The aluminum can was orange, so I assumed it was an orange drink. After drinking most of the Shandy within a few minutes, I began to feel a bit lightheaded. I looked at the can again, and realized that Shandy is a combination of orange drink and beer.

ACTIVITY 5.13

Use the preceding example to respond to the following.

1. How would you have felt if you had experienced the situation described in the previous example?

2. What cultural assumptions were made in this example?

3. What cultural differences are illustrated by this example?

Example: Comfort Food

I was in Malta for a two-week visit. Near the end of my trip, I got a bad cold and was feeling miserable. My appetite was minimal, and what I really wanted to eat was a lettuce salad. Dinners in Malta were typically four courses—appetizer, soup, entree and dessert. Lettuce was usually used only as a garnish for some dishes. Cheese was a dessert option. So I gathered my courage to talk to my server about my request. I asked for some lettuce, some tomato and some bleu cheese. I explained that I would be combining the ingredients. I also did my best to apologize for what I knew was an unusual request. The server complied, although he was obviously curious about the combination of foods and the fact that I wanted nothing else. Several staff members came to my table to see the concoction and to comment on its peculiarity. Even though I knew my server and other staff quite well because of my extended stay at the hotel, and they were very gracious in the situation, I was a bit uncomfortable with my lack of cultural fit. I was also surprised about the level of my need for the cultural "comfort food" I requested.

Food choices are sometimes determined by religion. Until a few decades ago, Catholics were not allowed to eat meat on Fridays. Jews must not eat pork. Hindus do not eat beef. Fasting is part of several religions. Japanese tea ceremonies have both leisure and spiritual connections. The following are a few examples of unintentional cultural insensitivity about food.

♦ Bread was highlighted during a university residence hall "theme meal." The event was during Jewish Passover, when eating bread is forbidden.

♦ An instructor brings chocolate candy to class as a treat for the students. Several students in the class could not eat it, because they gave up chocolate for Lent.

♦ A business luncheon for people working on a diversity initiative had one entree—a casserole of chicken and sausage in a cream and cheese sauce.

ACTIVITY 5.14

1. What types of foods and meals are most often included in your family?

2. What types of foods relate to your ethnicity?

3. Describe your family's eating patterns (e.g., everyone sitting down to dinner, eating separately).

4. What values do your family's eating patterns represent?

5. What are your comfort foods and their family/historical origins?

6. What foods are eaten by other cultures and found peculiar by you?

Clothing and Appearance

There are many examples around the world of clothing and appearance as having cultural significance. The significance can be based on religion or other cultural factors. For example, the wearing of the Yarmulke by Jewish men, beards for married men in some religions and the veiling of women by Muslims all reflect religious practices. The veiling of women is considered to be a sign of respect for women. In the United States, women in Catholic churches traditionally covered their head with chapel veils, scarves or hats until the practice was discontinued in the 1960s.

Clothing and appearance can reflect regional differences. In India, the way a sari is worn can indicate in what region of India a woman lives. Adrinka cloth in African cultures identifies regions and has other cultural significance. A cowboy hat in the United States is more likely to be seen in Texas or Montana than New York or Vermont.

The aesthetics of beauty vary culturally and over time. While the binding of women's feet in China or flattening of the forehead in African tribes might seem inhumane or unnecessary, body sculpting, body piercing (including ear piercing) and tattooing might seem acceptable. Male circumcision, done for religious reasons in some circumstances and considered inhumane in some cultures, has been widely practiced in the United States.

In Asian dress, clothing such as saris and kimonos are often unstructured or rectangular. The shape of the garment comes from the way the garment is put on the body. Clothing in Europe and the United States is often cut to provide shape and structure on the body through the garment. From hoop skirts to corsets to shoulder pads, garments have historically reflected the aesthetics of women's beauty.

What body image and body type is ideal varies from culture to culture. In the United States, the ideal is for men to be tall and women to be thin. San Francisco has passed an ordinance prohibiting discrimination on the basis of weight. Although not the first community to pass such an ordinance, the San Francisco ordinance was well publicized throughout the country and served to generate discussion about body size as an issue of diversity.

ACTIVITY 5.15

1. Describe your clothing style.

2. What factors influence your clothing style?

3. What values does your clothing style represent?

4. What is the unspoken dress code of your university?

5. What values does the university's unspoken dress code represent?

6. What are some other appearance characteristics (e.g., hair, body piercing, tattooing)?

7. Describe a "culture" and its associated dress and appearance characteristics (e.g., "biker" culture, cultures of musical styles).

8. Describe a type of appearance and the stereotypes about a person exhibiting that type.

Holidays and Associated Rituals

Holidays and associated rituals are often related to race, ethnicity, religion or some other aspect of diversity. They also often include elements of many characteristics of culture, such as food and eating patterns, and leisure and recreation.

Holidays are a useful way to both identify and understand underlying values and make connections to other diversity issues. For example, legal recognition of Martin Luther King Day has been controversial in many states. Jewish employees have often had difficulty in getting time off to celebrate important religious holidays. Public schools have grappled with issues of both religious holidays and people opposed to the observance of Halloween.

ACTIVITY 5.16

1. What is the most important holiday to you?

2. What characteristics and systems of culture are part of the holiday?

3. How is the holiday celebrated?

4. What rituals are common to people celebrating the holiday?

5. Does everyone in your culture (as you define it) celebrate this holiday the same way? Why are there differences?

6. What are holidays and celebrations that are unique to your college or university?

7. What are the underlying cultural values of those holidays and celebrations?

8. List as many national and global holidays and celebrations as you can (e.g., Mardi Gras, Cinco de Mayo). For each, list the most important system or characteristics of culture associated with the holiday or tradition.

Example: Kwanzaa

Kwanzaa (meaning "the first fruits") is a seven-day cultural celebration (December 26 through January 1) begun by Dr. Maulana Karenga in 1966. The celebration is designed to help those of African descent and others think about the historical roots and present-day lives of Africans and their descendants. Kwanzaa is not a religious holiday. The celebration includes rituals and traditional colors: black (for the faces of African American people and for unity), red (for the blood shed by people) and green (for hope and color of the motherland). At the heart of the Kwanzaa celebration are the following seven principles. The language of the principles is Swahili.

1. Umoja (unity) (oo-MOE-jah)—To strive for and maintain unity in the family, community, nation and race.

2. Kujichagulia (self-determination) (koo-jee-cha-goo-LEE-ah)—To define ourselves, name ourselves, create for ourselves and speak for ourselves.

3. Ujima (collective works and responsibility) (oo-JEE-mah)—To build and maintain our community together and to make our brothers' and sisters' problems our problems and to solve them together.

4. Ujamaa (cooperative economics) (oo-JAH-mah)—To build and maintain our own stores, shops and other businesses and to profit together from them.

5. Nia (purpose) (nee-AH)—To make as our collective vocation the building and developing of our community in order to restore our people to their traditional greatness.

6. Kuumba (creativity) (koo-OOM-bah)—To do always as much as we can, in the way that we can, in order to leave our community more beautiful and beneficial than when we inherited it.

7. Imani (faith) (ee-MAH-nee)—To believe with all our hearts in our parents, our teachers, our leaders, our people and the righteousness and victory of our struggle.

ACTIVITY 5.17

Use the preceding example to respond to the following.

1. Have you ever celebrated Kwanzaa? Why or why not?

2. Have you ever celebrated a cultural tradition that is not part of your personal ethnicity (e.g., St. Patrick's Day)? Why or why not?

3. Were you familiar with the principles of Kwanzaa before reading them here?

4. What values and beliefs are inherent in the seven principles of Kwanzaa?

5. How similar or dissimilar to your values and beliefs is each of the principles of Kwanzaa? Give examples.

6. Why do you think Kwanzaa was developed as a cultural tradition?

7. What is your opinion of cultural holidays and traditions such as Kwanzaa?

Conceptual Framework to Explore Diversity Understanding: Systems of Culture

"The first key to wisdom is this—constant and frequent questioning . . . for by doubting, we are led to question and by questioning we arrive at the truth."

Peter Abelard

"It is not healthy when a nation lives within a nation, as colored Americans are living inside America. A nation cannot live confident of its tomorrow if its refugees are among its own citizens."

Pearl S. Buck, *What America Means to Me*, 1942

Objectives of Chapter 6

The overall objective of Chapter 6 is to identify and explore examples of systems of culture as a way to understand cultural differences and similarities. Specific objectives for the chapter follow.

❖ Examine education in culture
❖ Understand the role of family and kinship patterns in culture
❖ Explore religion in culture
❖ Identify political issues in culture
❖ Examine economic issues in culture
❖ Discuss the linkages between systems of culture

Characteristics and Systems of Culture

In this chapter, some major systems of culture will be described. Case examples and activities will be used to increase understanding of how systems of culture can increase cultural understanding.

It should be noted that although this chapter will focus on systems individually, there are often strong relationships between different systems and between characteristics and systems. Those relationships will be examined in the more complex case examples in Chapter 7. It should also be noted that the systems selected for discussion represent a sampling rather than a complete list.

Education

There are many cultural differences in education. The journalistic framework of "who, what, when, where and how" is a useful way of exploring dimensions of education.

Who

Who is educated in a culture? In the United States, all children have a legal right to formal public school education from kindergarten through high school, although there are many issues about the level of equality in public education. In other cultures, gender, social status, income or other factors limit K–12 formal education.

ACTIVITY 6.1

1. Do you believe K–12 education should be a right for all children in the United States?

2. Is K–12 education equal for all children in the United States? Discuss your answer.

ACTIVITY 6.2

1. Identify as many issues as you can related to university admissions policies.

2. Describe "ideal" diversity in a college or university.

3. What types of diversity are most important to include in your ideal? Why?

4. What types of diversity are least important to include in your ideal? Why?

5. In what ways can the college or university work to achieve your ideal?

6. What are your college or university's perceptions of the "ideal"? How are the perceptions similar or dissimilar to your own perceptions?

7. Who sets the standards in your college or university? How are the standards defined?

8. Who benefits from the standards? Who does not benefit?

In universities in the United States, who gets to attend is a question often tackled by admissions offices and others in the university. Who is allowed to attend and who is turned away is complex and often misunderstood and controversial. (For more information, *The Shape of the River* by William G. Bowen and Derek Curtis Bok provides the most comprehensive examination to date of university admissions and affirmative action policies.)

Example: Education

A boy in Alabama was diagnosed as disabled because of severe behavioral problems that began at an early age. At age 16, his disruptive behavior in school included threats to teachers and students, fighting, spitting, obscene language and drawings depicting killing other people. A teacher's aide was hired to sit with him in class and another aide was hired to ride the school bus, where the student had threatened to cause an accident.

The local district attorney led an effort to permanently expel the student from all public schools in Alabama. The mother of the student sued, stating that the student had a right to a public education.

ACTIVITY 6.3

Use the preceding example to respond to the following.

1. What are the rights of the student diagnosed as disabled?

2. How should those individual rights be balanced with the rights of other students, teachers and staff?

3. Who should pay for the costs?

4. What are possible solutions to this situation?

WHAT

What does a student have a right to learn? Even in cultures that have formal education available to most children, that answer varies. For example, in England, "O-level" (ordinary) and "A-level" (advanced) examinations determine whether students will be trained for a technical or professional career, and whether or not their education will continue beyond a certain point. In Japan, test scores from the elementary grade levels may determine children's futures.

Gender often limits what a student can learn. In some cultures, girls are not allowed to be educated at all. In other cases, what they learn is limited. Even in the United States, girls and boys may be steered toward or away from certain areas. For example, non-college-bound girls may be encouraged to take secretarial training. Boys with aptitude and interest in this area may be discouraged from pursuing similar training. This type of steering creates gender bias for the fields of study, as well as limiting career options for both boys and girls.

The right to post-secondary education varies widely around the world. In many cultures, a university education is reserved for the privileged few. In the United States, there is an assumption that anyone can go to college if he or she works hard enough. In practice, however, there are many limiting factors, including socioeconomic status, inequality in funding of public schools, unequal preparation of students for college and tracking of students, among others.

ACTIVITY 6.4

1. How common is attending college in the United States?

2. Is attending college a right in the United States?

3. Does everyone have equal access to college in the United States?

4. What is your reason for attending college?

5. What societal values, beliefs and assumptions are inherent in post-secondary education in the United States?

6. In what ways are teaching and learning in the United States impacted by racism, sexism and other types of differential treatment based on diversity? Make a list by type of diversity. Be sure to include access, quality and other important issues.

WHEN

When do children attend school? Currently, children are usually five or six years old when starting school. Why has the age moved higher? One reason is that many children now attend preschool programs beginning at age three. So what appears to be a higher age for the beginning of formal education is for many a lower age.

The traditional age for attending college in the United States is between 18 and 22 years of age. Colleges have varying percentages of non-traditional students. The percentage often varies by location (e.g., urban campuses), type of college (e.g., "branch" campus) and support services, among other factors.

ACTIVITY 6.5

1. What is the percentage of nontraditional-aged students at your institution?

2. What characteristics of your school welcome or do not welcome nontraditional-aged students (e.g., time schedule of classes)?

3. How is a classroom enhanced (or not) by nontraditional-aged students?

4. Is age diversity an important goal for your university? Why or why not?

5. Should age diversity be an important goal for your university? Why or why not?

WHERE

Issues in K–12 education in the United States related to where a child attends school include private versus public schools, home schooling, inequality of funding in public schools and bussing of students, among others. School vouchers, school accountability and other current topics are related to those issues.

Status of schools is another factor related to where education occurs. In some cultures, boarding schools away from home are common for upper-income children, even in elementary school grade levels.

ACTIVITY 6.6

1. What are your opinions about the issues listed in the previous paragraphs?

2. How do your cultural beliefs and values influence your opinions?

HOW

How children are taught obviously overlaps with dimensions of the "who, what, where and when" of education. Issues related to how children are taught include learning styles and teaching techniques, formal schooling versus self-teaching, why learning is valued and what kind of learning is valued (e.g., critical thinking, memorization). Some cultures highly value story-telling and oral history to teach children. Native American Indian, African-American and Appalachian cultures in the United States are a few examples.

Activity 6.7

1. List cultural issues related to how people are taught.

2. For each issue, describe the underlying cultural values.

3. Describe how methods of teaching and learning are valued or not valued in your culture.

Activity 6.8

1. In your family how is "best" defined in the United States in K–12 and post-secondary education (e.g., best education, best school, best program)?

2. How do you think your definition would differ from other groups of people within the United States? Why do the differences exist?

3. How do you think your definition would differ from other groups of people globally? Why do the differences exist?

4. What are other controversial educational issues in your culture?

5. How does the education system in your culture vary from other cultures? Give examples.

6. How did you pick the school you are attending? What values entered into your decision?

Family and Kinship Patterns

Family and kinship patterns are highly complex and are both individually and culturally variable. A few basic elements of family will be discussed in this section as a way to illustrate cultural differences and similarities. Specifically, the chapter will focus on defining family; dating, courtship and marriage; and parenting.

Defining Family

Defining family is a difficult task. The nuclear family (mother, father, and children) excludes many types of families, including single parent families, extended families, blended families, single-person families, same-sex cou-

ples and families without children present, to name just a few.

The decennial census conducted in the United States is a good example of how definitions of family are complex and have changed over time. In the 2000 census, information on each individual living in a household was gathered, including age, race, whether the person is Hispanic, and relationship to the first person listed in the household information. Designating a "head of household," common in censuses until a few decades ago was not part of the 2000 census. Removing the head of household designator was a response to changing gender roles and family types.

ACTIVITY **6.9**

1. What does a "typical" family in the United States look like? Be as specific as possible in your description.

2. Does your family represent the "typical"? Why or why not?

3. Give examples of types of "nontypical" families. Why do they exist?

DATING, COURTSHIP AND MARRIAGE

How a mate (or mates) is (are) selected is an important part of family patterns. Dating and courtship patterns vary widely both within the United States and around the world. Age of dating and marriage, how and by whom mates are selected, cultural views on gay and lesbian marriage and the role of romantic love are both individually and culturally variable.

ACTIVITY **6.10**

1. In your culture, what is the ideal age to start dating?

2. In your culture, what is the ideal age to get married?

3. Speculate about the reasons why the ideals you gave are the best ages.

4. What are some examples of cultures with different ideal ages? What are some examples of generations with different age ideals?

5. Speculate about the reasons why the differences exist in the examples of cultures you described.

6. What is the purpose of marriage?

7. Do you believe in love at first sight?

8. How important is romantic love in selecting a mate? What other factors might be important? Why?

9. List advantages and disadvantages of self-selecting a mate.

10. List advantages and disadvantages of arranged marriages.

11. List and discuss perspectives on gay and lesbian marriage.

The following are examples of views on dating, courtship and marriage. They reflect many issues, including self-selection versus arranged marriages, age, gay and lesbian marriage and gender.

Examples: Dating, Courtship and Marriage

Example #1

Two families had separate traveling evangelical Christian ministries that served several states in the United States. Each family had a teenage child. The families, who knew each other only slightly, arranged a marriage between the teenagers. The teenage children corresponded through letters during the year before the marriage. After the couple was married, the wife lived with her husband's family, seeing her own family only rarely while traveling.

Example #2

Pradeep is a United States citizen in his late 20s. His parents moved to the United States when Pradeep was a child. He attended public schools and a prestigious college. After completing his Ph.D., his parents encouraged him to marry. Most of Pradeep's friends are of European-American descent. He dates casually, but has not had a serious relationship. His parents want him to marry an Indian woman from the same social status as his family. He has difficulty explaining the concept of arranged marriage to his friends, and begins to doubt whether or not he wants to marry through an arranged marriage. His mother gets Pradeep to agree to meetings with several young Indian women, many of whom also grew up in the United States. He travels throughout the United States and India during a two-year period, meeting women and their chaperons. Finally, a decision is made. He marries Sarah, a Ph.D. chemist who is also Indian. Pradeep and Sarah met briefly three times before the wedding.

Example #3

Mary Jo Leterneau, a sixth-grade teacher and married mother of four children, had a sexual relationship with one of her students. Leterneau gave birth to a child fathered by the student. She was convicted of statutory rape. While out of jail, she violated a court order not to see the student, and became pregnant with another child. Leterneau is currently serving her prison sentence.

Example #4

A lesbian couple is married through a church. They send formal invitations to their friends and families.

ACTIVITY 6.11

Use the preceding examples to respond to the following.

1. When exploring self-selection versus arranged marriages, compare and contrast the cultural issues possible in examples one and two on the previous page.

2. Assume you want to marry someone, but your parents and friends do not approve. What is the impact of parent and friend approval on your decision? How does that approval relate to the underlying assumptions of arranged marriages?

3. Describe the cultural issues in the Leterneau case.

4. How do you feel about gay and lesbian marriages? What questions would you have if you were invited to a gay or lesbian ceremony?

Legal constraints on marriage are useful in identifying cultural values. In the United States, a person can be married to only one person at a time, making polygamy (more than one wife) and polyandry (more than one husband) illegal. States have varying minimum ages for marriage.

Although many gay and lesbian couples have church weddings, most states ban the legal recognition of same-sex marriages. In spring 2000, Vermont passed legislation legalizing civil-union licenses for same-sex couples, including some legal rights associated with marriage. At around the same time, California voters went in the other direction, banning the legal recognition of same-sex marriages, including those performed legally in other states.

Historically, interracial marriages were banned in the United States in many states. People with disabilities, such as mental retardation, were also often prevented from marrying.

Examples: Polygamy and Polyandry

Example #1

In Utah, there are still examples of extended polygamous (one husband, multiple wives) families, although the Church of Jesus Christ and Latter Day Saints no longer sanctions polygamy. The polygamy is based on the religious beliefs of the church. There are cases where a man will marry sisters from the same family. Age of marriage for women is often mid-teens. Prosecution of polygamous families is rare, but a recent case involving Utah polygamist Tom Green and his five wives resulted in his prosecution.

Example #2

A female student is attending a few college classes while her husband finishes an advanced degree. They are from an African country where polygamy is allowed, and plan to return after completion of the husband's studies. They have a three-year-old child, and the wife is pregnant with their second child. She complains that her husband has become "Westernized" and is reluctant to take a second wife upon returning to their country. She expects him to have multiple wives. As the first wife, she will have lifetime privilege in the family, as her mother did before her. The second and subsequent wives will lessen her workload in household duties and childcare.

Example #3

Polyandry (one wife, multiple husbands) is much rarer than polygamy in the world. Instances of polyandry are usually found where people are living in harsh conditions where population must be strictly controlled.

ACTIVITY 6.12

Use the preceding examples to answer the following questions.

1. What is your opinion about polygamy and polyandry?

1. What are the underlying reasons for polygamy and polyandry?

2. Why is polygamy more common in world cultures than polyandry?

3. Why are polygamy and polyandry not part of the dominant culture in the United States?

PARENTING PRACTICES

Parenting practices also vary culturally. Whether or not to have children, when to have children, how many children to have, reproductive rights, the relationship of childbearing to religion, spacing of children and parenting practices are a few examples of culturally variable issues related to parenting. There are many specific examples of these issues, including China's one-child policy, birth control and abortion, interracial adoptions, international adoptions and adoptions by gay couples, among others.

Examples: Issues of Birth Control, Conception and Adoption

Example #1

During a visit to Malta, a country whose population is almost entirely Catholic, I noticed that most families were small, with one or two children. I also knew that birth control devices, including condoms, were not available at that time in the country because of the predominance of Catholicism.

One of my friends was a young Maltese woman. I asked her how Maltese families were so successful in controlling family size without birth control. She laughingly replied that in Malta, the only way to get birth control pills was if a woman had a gynecological problem. She continued her explanation by saying that most married women in Malta had gynecological problems.

Example #2

Two couples (one White and one Black) were undergoing fertility treatments at a well-respected clinic. One couple conceived twins. When the babies were delivered, one child was White and the other was Black. DNA tests confirmed that the fertilized egg of the Black couple was erroneously implanted into the White woman who gave birth to the twins. So, although both children had been born at the same time to one mother, the twins were not biologically related, nor was the Black twin biologically related to the birth mother or her husband. A legal custody battle ensued. Eventually, the Black family was awarded their biological child, with visitation rights awarded to the White parents.

Example #3

A 56-year-old woman underwent fertility treatments. She gave birth to a baby. In early 2000, a 53-year old woman in the United States gave birth to triplets; she had no fertility drugs or treatment to induce conception.

Example #4

A woman with a severe and genetically linked mental disorder is sterilized without her consent at the long-term treatment facility where she lives.

Example #5

Some states have passed legislation banning adoption by same-sex couples.

ACTIVITY 6.13

Use the preceding examples to respond to the following.

1. What are the cultural assumptions and values in the preceding examples?

2. How and why are the assumptions variable from culture to culture (or from individual to individual)?

Examples: Child Care

Example #1

A woman from Denmark was visiting her boyfriend in New York City. The couple went to a local restaurant for dinner, leaving their infant child outside the restaurant in a baby carriage. Alarmed people on the street contacted the police, who arrived and arrested the mother for abandoning her baby.

The response of the mother was disbelief. She let the police know that in Denmark, it was common practice to leave small children outside of restaurants, and that she was able to maintain visual contact with the baby from her table. Her lawyer used differences in culture as part of her legal defense. The father of the baby was not charged with a crime.

Example #2

In Malta, a friend from the United States asks a young mother about who cares for children. Most young mothers do not work for several years after a child is born in Malta. The term "baby-sitter" was unfamiliar to the mother, even in the case of running errands or going out for an evening with her husband. When the American explained that a baby-sitter, often a teenage girl, cares for a child when the parents cannot, the mother was aghast at the concept. "Do you mean to tell me that in the United States, people leave their children, the most important people in their lives, in the care of a 15- or 16-year-old child and with total strangers for day care?" "Yes," the American replied. "Sometimes the baby-sitters are even younger than 15." The mother went on to describe how in Malta, only a family member would be allowed the enormous responsibility of caring for a child. Further, children are with parents whenever possible, and it is not uncommon to see them at restaurants, entertainment events or anywhere else.

ACTIVITY 6.14

Use the preceding example to respond to the following.

1. What are the cultural assumptions in the preceding examples?

2. How and why are the assumptions variable from culture to culture (or from individual to individual)?

Religion

Variations in religion and faith are often a source of misunderstanding and conflict between people and cultures. Conflicts in Northern Ireland, between Palistinians and Israelis, between India and Pakistan, and in the former Yugoslavia in Eastern Europe are just a few examples of global conflict based in part on religious differences.

Religion often has strong interrelationships with other characteristics and systems of culture. For example, religious bans on birth control may affect average family size. Religious beliefs may limit foods that can be eaten, clothing that can be worn or activities, among other things.

Although Christianity is the dominant religion in the United States, it is the religion for only about one-third of the world population. Muslims represent nearly one-fifth of the world population, followed by Hindus (13%), Buddhists (6%), and Jews (less than one percent). Over one-fifth of the world population is non-religious or atheist, and nearly 10% represent religions other than those previously listed.

ACTIVITY 6.15

1. What was the dominant religion in the community (or communities) where you grew up?

2. How did your "fit" in the dominant religious culture affect you (e.g., if you were part of the dominant culture, not part of the dominant culture, atheist, agnostic)?

3. How do your religious beliefs vary from those of other cultures? Give examples.

4. Describe examples of how your religious beliefs impact on other cultural systems in your life.

Example: Religion

A Christian man wishes to attend meetings of a Jewish singles club. When he calls to inquire about meeting times, he is told that the meetings are only for Jewish people and that he should not attend. He responds that he is not prejudiced about religion, and that if he is not allowed to participate in the meetings, then the Jewish participants are prejudiced against him.

ACTIVITY **6.16**

Use the preceding example to respond to the following.

1. What is your initial reaction to this example?

2. How is your initial reaction influenced by your own religious beliefs?

3. What values might be likely for each of the individuals in the example?

Additional information: The population of Jewish people in Europe was significantly decreased during the Holocaust. Many Jewish people are afraid their race/culture/religion is dying because so many Jews are marrying gentiles. In Jewish law and custom, a Jewish man who marries a gentile woman will have gentile children, unless they convert. When a Jewish woman marries a gentile man, the children are considered to be Jewish.

4. How does the previous information support or change your initial viewpoint?

5. What gender issues are involved here?

Politics

The role of politics as a system of culture is multidimensional and highly related to other characteristics and systems of culture. Most local, regional, national and global news events and current issues have connections to political values and policies. This section will focus on three political concepts with relationships to diversity awareness, understanding and synthesis: (a) balancing dominant and nondominant perspectives, (b) understanding the roles of local, state and federal politics within the United States and (c) analyzing global events using politics as a system of culture.

BALANCING DOMINANT AND NONDOMINANT PERSPECTIVES

The notion that democracy is based on majority rule makes for interesting and ongoing debates in the United States about balancing the wishes of the majority with the rights of minorities. Immigration policies, anti-discrimination legislation (e.g., Civil Rights Act of 1964, Americans with Disabilities Act of 1990),

and policies related to rights for all people in the United States (e.g., public school education, free speech) are examples of major political initiatives and underpinnings of United States politics.

There are many specific issues that relate to how balancing democracy and nondominant perspectives reflect societal values. For example, the rights of people who are poor for food, shelter, housing, and employment lead to minimal welfare and minimum wage policies. Some nondominant groups are less protected from discrimination than others—there is more legislation related to race, ethnicity and gender, for example, than for sexual orientation.

The treatment of Native American Indian people in the United States provides another example of the difficulties in balancing majority and minority rights. Historically, tribal rights and sovereignty issues have attempted to provide that balance. However, history has shown that rights of Native American Indians have been considerably reduced or eliminated. Current legal issues for Native American Indians reflect a continuation of that pattern.

ACTIVITY 6.17

1. List adjectives that you believe are part of democracy (e.g., freedom, equality).

2. Using the list of adjectives, describe challenges for each.

3. Give examples (in addition to those listed above) of policies designed to include non-dominant perspectives.

4. For each example you have included, describe the underlying societal values.

5. Give examples of specific issues or events (in addition to those listed above) in the news that relate to balancing dominant and nondominant perspectives.

LOCAL, STATE AND FEDERAL POLITICS

A major political issue in the United States is the balance between local, state and federal control. Local politics often affect day-to-day living (e.g., school levies, availability and quality of services). Advocates of local and state control argue that more local control can better respond to the individual needs of communities and states. Advocates of more federal control suggest that the needs of the nation as a whole sometimes require federal involvement.

A recent example of conflict in the rights of states is the debate in South Carolina about the display of the Confederate flag on the state Capitol building. The South Carolina legislature initially voted to maintain the display of the flag, citing the importance of the flag to the history of the state. Opponents of the flag argued it was a symbol of South Carolina's racist past. Although no federal legislation prevented the display, public pressure from around the country escalated to remove the flag. Economic boycotts of the state included groups canceling major conferences in South Carolina. The pressure eventually led to removal of the flag from the Capitol building.

Another example of a current state versus federal issue that will continue to escalate as the percentage of Spanish-speaking people in the United States increases is the "English-only" debate. This is an interesting debate because in most countries being multilingual is considered an asset. Although some states have been passing English-only legislation, there is no Supreme Court or federal legislation to date. The English-only debate may be the next big battle between states and the federal government. It might be similar to the civil rights movement, where some states did not ban discrimination, and fought the passage of federal legislation.

A third current state versus federal issue involves gay marriages and civil unions. In 1996, federal legislation was passed that defines marriage as between a man and a woman. The legislation, entitled the Defense of Marriage Act (DOMA), also provides that no state shall be required to recognize laws of other states regarding same-sex marriage. As discussed elsewhere in this book, many states have passed legislation banning same-sex marriage, same-sex adoption, and other rights for gay couples. In addition, at the time of this writing, an amendment to the United States Constitution is being discussed that calls for ". . . defining and protecting marriage as a union of man and woman as husband and wife. The amendment should fully protect marriage, while leaving the state legislatures free to make their own choices in defining legal arrangements other than marriage" (George W. Bush, February 24, 2004).

Activity 6.18

1. What is your opinion of the "English-only" debate?

2. What are the issues involved in the debate?

3. What are the benefits of a multilingual country?

4. What are the limitations of a multilingual country?

5. What are the cultural values of the United States that support multilingualism?

6. What are the cultural values of the United States that do not support multilingualism?

Example: Local Politics

In a Midwestern city with a population of around 100,000, a city councilwoman proposed a human rights ordinance for the city. The ordinance was designed to go beyond federal and state protections for people in the areas of housing, public transportation and employment. Most of the ordinance was popular with a majority of people in the city, many of whom could benefit from the protection provided. However, there was one protected class of people within the ordinance that created controversy—homosexuals. Under the ordinance, homosexuals could not be discriminated against in renting or buying housing, in access to or use of local public transportation, and in hiring and employment retention.

On Election Day, there was a substantially higher voter turnout than usual. In one polling place, an elderly woman walked slowly to a voting booth. She entered the booth and closed the curtain around her. People across the room heard her loudly shout "No!" as she pulled the voting lever. She exited the booth and the polling station.

The human rights ordinance was overwhelmingly defeated. It was clear that the inclusion of gay rights was a deal breaker for many voters who would have otherwise supported the ordinance. The city councilwoman, an ex-nun who had served several terms in Council, lost her next election.

ACTIVITY 6.19

Use the preceding example to respond to the following.

1. How does the example relate to the issue of majority versus nondominant group rights?

2. How can rights of smaller groups be protected in a majority rules system?

3. How does the example relate to issues of local politics?

4. What are the responsibilities of politicians to serve all of their constituents?

5. List the advantages and disadvantages of local and state control.

6. List the advantages and disadvantages of federal control.

ANALYZING WORLD EVENTS USING POLITICAL SYSTEMS

Political systems and processes are often at the heart of world events. Because of differences in political systems, it is often difficult to understand world events. The ethnocentrism of viewing an event from a democracy point of view sometimes contributes to a more limited understanding. The following are examples of issues. After each issue, a list of factors that could contribute to cultural misunderstanding is included. These factors represent cultural differences we might not be aware of if we examine the issues through our own cultural lens.

♦ *Issue:* Joerg Haider was elected to a coalition government in Austria in early 2000. Haider had expressed views that were considered to be sympathetic to Nazis during World War II. Public opposition to his election led to sanctions by the European community, and debates about the rights of Austria versus rights of Europe. Haider eventually resigned.

Factors: Austria is socialist; differences in coalition government structure; significance of World War II in Europe; size and relationship of European countries

♦ *Issue:* Slavery throughout the world is a current issue as well as a historical one. In *Disposable People: New Slavery in the Global Economy,* Kevin Bales estimates there are 27 million people worldwide in chattel slavery, debt bondage or contract slavery. A United States CIA/State Department report published in spring 2000 estimates that 50,000 women and children are being held as slaves in the sex trade in the United States. These women and children are often lured from Eastern Europe, Russia and Asia with promises of jobs.

Factors: Economic conditions in many countries; economic incentives for slavery; gender issues

♦ *Issue:* The Chinese government enacted a national policy that prohibited families from having more than one child. Abortion and sterilization are encouraged. Permits to have a child must be obtained. Serious sanctions are imposed on families that have more than one child.

Factors: Projected consequences of population growth; political and cultural emphasis on the rights of the population as a whole versus individual rights

---

ACTIVITY **6.20**

1. Identify a list of current global issues.

2. For each, summarize the issue and "cultural lens" factors that might affect interpretation of the issue.

Economics

The role of economics as a system of culture is very broad and highly related to other characteristics and systems of culture. This section will focus on three economic concepts with relationships to diversity awareness, understanding and synthesis: (a) the competitive market model, (b) links between the economic system, poverty and discrimination in the United States and (c) the effects of economics on global issues.

THE COMPETITIVE MARKET MODEL

The competitive market model is the basis for the economy in the United States and is based on several assumptions. A key assumption with implications for diversity is that there is no discrimination.

There are many examples of discrimination related to economics in the United States. For example, women and people of color are paid less than White men for equivalent work; the unemployment rate for people actively seeking employment is higher for people of color and people with disabilities; the elderly and people of color are more likely to live in substandard housing; and female and minority business owners are less likely to get construction and other types of contracts.

A more detailed examination of one type of violation of the competitive market model assumption—housing discrimination—illustrates constraints often experienced by people of color. It is well documented that housing discrimination exists and takes many forms. In the rental market, landlords often misrepresent the availability of rental units and charge higher deposit and monthly rental fees for people of color.

In home ownership, discriminatory practices include steering and redlining. Steering is a real estate practice where an agent or broker provide different lists of available properties to potential buyers based on race, ethnicity, or religion. Redlining is a mortgage lending practice where loans on individual houses are turned down because of the condition of the neighborhood in which they are located.

Although the types of housing discrimination described above are illegal, they (and others) still exist. The effects of discriminatory practices on individuals and families are obvious. The effects on neighborhoods and communities is also significant, including deterioration of housing stock because of redlining, lost sales of properties because of racial steering or other restrictions and losses to local businesses, among others.

LINKS BETWEEN THE ECONOMIC SYSTEM, POVERTY AND DISCRIMINATION IN THE UNITED STATES

There are several links between the economic system, poverty and discrimination in the United States. The first is the cultural interpretation of work ethic. The work ethic in the United States suggests that if you work hard, you will succeed. If you succeed, you will make money. If you make money, you will not be poor. Therefore, if you are poor, you do not work hard.

Activity 6.21

1. What are some examples of people who work hard and do not make a lot of money (e.g., college students, migrant workers, people working for minimum wage)?

2. What are some examples of people who make a lot of money (or have a lot of money) but may not work hard (e.g., people who inherit money, people who have money they have gotten illegally)?

3. What values are inherent in the cultural interpretation of work ethic?

4. Data from the 2000 census indicate that median household income for Black families is around $28,000. The median income for White families is around $40,000. Why is there a difference? Speculate about as many reasons as you can.

5. What kinds of barriers exist to the economic success of people?

Activity 6.22

1. Calculate monthly living expenses for a household of three people (two adults and one elementary school-aged child). Be sure to include estimates for clothing, food, housing, health insurance, car expenses, school expenses, entertainment, etc. Make your list of expenses as complete and accurate as possible.

2. Calculate the minimum gross income required to meet the monthly living expenses you have outlined. Assume that taxes (federal, state and local) will be about 25% of the income.

3. Using the income and expense projections, describe the kinds of employment situations that would allow the family to meet their expenses, and the kinds of employment that would not.

The work ethic relationship to perception of poverty in the United States is that people who are poor are usually doing something wrong. There are many stereotypes about the poor (e.g., lazy, stupid). A recent distinction in language is the use of the term "working poor" to refer to people who work at low-paying jobs that do not provide enough income for even minimal living expenses.

A second link between economics and discrimination is the relationship between class (or status) and wealth. People with less money (or in some cases fewer material manifestations of wealth) are more likely to be labeled as lower class, even though there are often news stories of people who have lived modest lives in low-paying jobs who make major donations to universities and charities after their deaths.

ACTIVITY 6.23

1. In what ways do people in the United States show wealth?

2. How does display of wealth in the United States differ from other cultures (be specific about what cultures)?

3. Give your first impressions of the following:

   a. a surgeon who lives in a small apartment in a modest neighborhood

   b. a garbage man who drives a late model luxury car

   c. a teenager in a low-income neighborhood who wears $200 athletic shoes

   d. a young mother with six children in a department store purchasing several expensive children's outfits

4. What attributes did you give to the people in the previous question? How are societal values represented in the connections between wealth, materialism and class?

A third link between economic systems, poverty and discrimination is the historical context of how wealth was built in the United States. Wealth was often acquired through the acquisition of property. For example, in the early 1900s my paternal grandparents became farmers in northwestern Iowa. My grandfather received a section of land (160 acres) to farm. Land was given to thousands of families in exchange for the farmers raising crops that would be used to feed the increasing population. The land was extremely fertile, and most farmers of that time were able to comfortably raise and educate their children.

Most people who were not of European descent did not have the opportunities my grandparents had. An analogy to describe the lasting effects of such inequities, including immigrants and others entering the economy now, is a Monopoly game. A player who enters the game after a few hours does not have the same chance of success as players who entered the game at the beginning and acquired the "best" properties (or were allowed to move others such as Native American Indians or Mexicans, to get those properties). Coupled with the right to inheritance, where properties are handed down to the next generation, the opportunities for people entering the game are severely limited.

Linkages between Systems

The systems of culture described in this chapter can be useful in beginning to explain cultural differences. In many cases, multiple systems are linked. The following case example is helpful in exploring the interrelationships between systems.

Example: Systems of Culture

A high school student in Malta is preparing for college. He has applied to the architecture program at the University of Malta. He has always wanted to be an architect, and has worked hard in school to get the grades he needs to be admitted into the University. Very few people in Malta are accepted into the University, which is the only one in the country. It is considered highly prestigious in Malta to have a college education. Because of family obligations, it is not possible for the student to attend college in another country.

Several months after applying, the student is informed that he has been admitted to the University. However, he will not be allowed to enter the architecture program, which is under a moratorium prohibiting new students. The moratorium is the result of an analysis of the professional needs of the country. Projections for the future indicate a surplus of architects and a shortage of accountants. The student's acceptance into the university is contingent on his agreement to be admitted in the accountancy program. He begins the accountancy program in the fall.

ACTIVITY 6.24

Use the preceding example to respond to the following.

1. Would this example be likely to happen in the United States?

2. What factors influenced the choice of major for the Maltese student?

3. What factors influenced your choice of major?

4. What information do you need and questions would you like to ask to better understand this scenario?

5. Speculate about possible differences in the Maltese culture that might contribute to explaining this example.

To better understand the preceding example, the systems of culture framework can be used to explore the possible differences in the Maltese culture that can explain this scenario. Not everything fits neatly into a systems/characteristics of culture framework, but the framework can be a starting point for analysis, and can include dimensions beyond those listed and discussed in this chapter.

First, the educational system in Malta is explained in part by the size of the country (population of around 500,000 people). The relatively small population necessitates that the pool of various professional people is used efficiently to support the labor needs of the country.

Second, the economy of Malta is heavily dependent on tourism. Tourism and tourist-related businesses are growing, thus creating a need for more accountants. The small physical size of the country does not support the need for more architects, since new building projects are limited by the small amount of available land.

Third, the political history and structure of Malta influence the educational system. The admission requirements and small percentage of people who attend college are similar to the British system. Malta was a British colony for well over 100 years.

Case Studies in Exploring Characteristics and Systems of Culture

"What is important is to keep learning, to enjoy challenge, and to tolerate ambiguity. In the end there are no certain answers."

Martina Horner

"Idealistic and realistic are only separated by changing someone's mind."

Ananda Lewis, former MTV veejay

Objectives of Chapter 7

The overall objective of Chapter 7 is to increase diversity awareness and understanding by applying the systems and characteristics of culture conceptual framework to a variety of case studies, ranging from daily events to national and global issues. Specific objectives for the chapter follow.

❖ Use observation of daily events to increase awareness and understanding of diversity
❖ Use case examples from individuals and family to increase awareness and understanding of diversity
❖ Apply examples from media and popular culture to increase awareness and understanding of diversity
❖ Identify issues and resources using the Internet
❖ Apply national and global issues and events to increase awareness and understanding of diversity
❖ Examine a case study of a culture (Deaf culture) and apply the understanding of the culture to issues within the culture

The skills developed through using characteristics and systems of culture to assist in understanding diversity can be applied at many levels, from personal interactions to global events. The following are steps and examples of how to use characteristics and systems.

Using Observation of Daily Events to Increase Awareness and Understanding of Characteristics and Systems of Culture

INCREASING AWARENESS

Awareness of difference is a first step in understanding difference. Daily activities are an ideal source of exposure to an endless range of diversity applications. Daily activities provide repetition, a variety of types of diversity and better understanding of some types of diversity.

One semester in college I was enrolled in four art classes—two lecture art history courses, a drawing studio and watercolor painting. I found that being immersed in seeing things differently spilled over into all aspects of my life that semester. I looked at color and composition everywhere. Driving in a rural area, I became aware of how the changing light of late afternoon changed the colors on the cornfields. In my apartment, I began to notice how things were designed, from appliances to furniture to the moldings around the doors and windows. Proportion and scale, the impact of line, pattern, texture and color all took on new meaning.

The process of immersion I used in college to better my awareness of design can be applied to building awareness of diversity through daily activities. The effects of the process are parallel to the level of immersion—the greater the level of immersion and awareness the more-long lasting the effects will be.

INCREASING UNDERSTANDING

Once awareness is established, increasing understanding through analysis is possible. The purpose of analysis is not to determine a right or wrong in a given situation, but rather to speculate about possible meanings and interpretations. Speculating about the meaning of difference provides practice in examining multiple perspectives and in determining the benefits and limitations of each perspective. That practice in turn allows for deeper levels of analysis.

LIMITATIONS OF CHARACTERISTICS AND SYSTEMS OF CULTURE

In Chapters 5 and 6, characteristics and systems of culture were introduced as an organizing framework for greater awareness and understanding of cultural differences. In some observations of daily activities the type of diversity may be more significant than the role of characteristics and systems of culture. For example, noticing a discriminatory behavior based on race may not have a direct systems or characteristics connection. However, in some cases the type of diversity is more direct, but systems or characteristics may also be important. In other cases, the systems or characteristics may be the most important factors in understanding the situation and using type of diversity alone could lead to stereotypes or misunderstanding.

Using characteristics and systems of culture as a conceptual framework can provide useful information in some cases, but not all. Other conceptual frameworks might yield more or less insight depending on the situation. The choice and success of a framework is analogous to a camera lens. The breadth that is gained using a wide-angle lens is at the expense of the depth of detail obtainable by using a telephoto or close-up lens. The subject of the photograph determines which lens type is best. A wide-angle lens used on the forest can show the relationship of masses of trees, but not the delicate details of a leaf structure. The standard lens on a camera—a 52-mm—provides a balance of depth and breadth that is suitable for many types of photographs.

The characteristics and systems framework is like the standard lens. It is a useful tool for general analysis. It is a perfect conceptual choice for some situations, but is less ideal for others.

Examples: Increasing Diversity Understanding Through Day-to-Day Observations

Example #1

On a crowded sidewalk in a U.S. city that draws tourists from all over the world, a small group of young people approach an elderly couple walking in the opposite direction. The young people are laughing loudly and talking in a language that is not understood by the elderly couple. The young people do not yield to the right and seem unaware of the discomfort of the elderly couple as they pass.

1. How would you have felt in this situation if you were one of the young people?

2. How would you have felt in this situation if you were one of the elderly people?

3. What are the types of diversity represented in the example?

4. What are the characteristics of culture represented in the example?

5. How would the example be interpreted similarly or differently if the example were modified, with the group of young people being students from a United States college visiting a European country?

Example #2

You and 20 other students are having a professional dinner with a group of recruiters from a major business in your field. You notice that at the next table, one of the recruiters is holding his fork in one hand and his knife in the other hand throughout the meal. He does not put the fork down until his meal is finished. You also notice that he is scooping his peas onto his fork with his knife, and that the peas are on the back of the fork rather than on the slightly concave front.

1. What are your impressions of the behavior? Are your impressions positive or negative? Why?

2. Speculate about reasons for the behavior.

(Note for instructor: See Instructor's Guide.)

TRACKING DAILY EVENTS

Making notes of daily diversity observations for a few weeks is a valuable and not very time-consuming way to increase awareness and understanding through immersion. The following example illustrates the process.

Example: Journal of Daily Diversity Observations During a Vacation

Monday Day 1

Observation: On the airplane flight, the captain gives an introduction that is unlike any I have heard before. "Good morning everyone. I am Captain Jones and our copilot is Captain Smith. Our crew today is (captain lists the names of three crew members). They graduated the academy at the top of their class. We are very proud of them and they deserve your respect on this flight." The crew members are all African Americans. Two are female, the third is male.

Analysis: I have never heard an airplane crew introduced that way before. I wonder if they have had some problems on previous flights and if the problems were racial.

Tuesday Day 2

Observation: At the pool of the hotel where we are staying, there are several international visitors from a variety of countries. Throughout the day and evening, my daughter Brenna approaches several children in the pool who do not speak English. Brenna seems confused and the other children appear somewhat fearful.

In one case when Brenna approaches a child, the mother of the child tells me that her child does not speak English, only French. I tell her that Brenna will be talking French in elementary school the following year. The demeanor of the mother immediately changes from apologetic to animated and comfortable. We begin a discussion of the importance of second languages.

Analysis: I think about the importance of valuing the languages of others, how foreign languages were not stressed during my schooling, and the ethnocentrism of that perspective.

Wednesday Day 3

Observation: We are spending the morning at the pool. I notice a tall Black man in shorts approaching the pool area. I think about how few African Americans are staying at the hotel. Then I realize the man is picking up towels—he is a hotel employee. No one is speaking to him.

Analysis: I think back to a conference that I attended in Orlando three years earlier. The conference was about race and ethnicity; many of the 1000 attendees were African American and Asian American. Most guests at the pool were African American during that previous trip. Most spoke to the African-American employees of the hotel.

Thursday Day 4

Observation: A television show promoting area attractions is aired through the cable television system. A brief history of Orlando is included. The report states that in 1875, there were only 87 souls in Orlando.

While traveling by car throughout the area, I notice a road sign that says "entering Osceola County." The sign includes the image of a Native American Indian.

Analysis: I wonder how many Native American Indians lived in the area in 1875, and what happened to the culture.

Observation: I watched the promotional video again, more consciously focusing on representation of diversity. Over and over, the families enjoying the parks and other attractions were White, two-parent families with two children. Typically, the attractive parents were in their mid to late 30s, with children around 7 to 12 years old. There were few if any older people, people with disabilities, overweight people or single parents.

Analysis: I think about the message being sent to families who do not fit the marketing profile.

Friday Day 5

On the return trip home, we are waiting at a terminal during a layover in the Atlanta airport. A young well-dressed woman gives something to several people. It looks about the size of a business card. She approaches me, hands me a card and continues on to the next person. The card reads "Happy St. Patrick's Day! I am a deaf person. I'm offering you this handy Tool Key Chain that may be used for glasses, watches, computers and more for only $2.00. The proceeds help pay my educational and living expenses. May I interest you in one? May God Bless You! Thanks for your kindness!"

Analysis: I think about the controversy in the disability rights movement about this type of activity. I also think about the reactions of people in the terminal, ranging from discomfort to pity.

ACTIVITY 7.1

Use the preceding example to respond to the following.

1. Which example from the five days was the most interesting to you? Why?

2. What types of diversity are represented in the five examples?

3. Keep a journal of your own diversity observations. What types of diversity are represented? What types of diversity are missing? How can you increase your awareness of multiple diversities?

4. What systems and characteristics are represented in the examples from your observations?

Activity 7.2

1. Select a photograph or set of photographs from a place. Make sure that there is nothing in the photograph(s) that explicitly says where it is.

2. Exchange pictures with a partner.

3. From the images of the place, speculate about the following:

   a. What it the climate?

   b. What is the geography?

   c. What activities take place there?

   d. What are the people like?

   e. What else do you know about the place?

4. Think about and respond to why you answered the questions the way you did. What were the cultural clues the pictures provided?

5. Learn the location of the place from your partner.

6. As a group, discuss the following:

   a. How we learn about places from visual cues.

   b. What cultural assumptions we make about places based on visual cues.

Activity 7.3

1. Describe the physical characteristics of your campus.

2. In what ways do the physical characteristics of your campus reflect your culture? What parts of your culture are not reflected in the physical characteristics?

3. In what ways do the physical characteristics of your campus reflect institutional culture?

4. With which aspects of the institutional culture are you the most comfortable? Why?

5. With which aspects of the institutional culture are you the least comfortable? Why?

Using Case Examples of Individuals and Families to Increase Awareness and Understanding of Characteristics and Systems of Culture

Friends and family can provide many examples to increase awareness and understanding of characteristics and systems of culture. The key is to think about people and examples from your life as a starting point. Using examples familiar to you will help you build skills that can be applied to national and global understanding.

Example: The Sinkonnens

When Paavo and Seija Sinkonnen arrived in the United States from Finland in the early 1970s, they brought the starter for a family recipe of sourdough rye bread. The starter was in their family for many years, and required keeping a bit of the dough for the next loaf. If the starter was gone, the bread could not be made. When they went through customs, the customs agent did not know what it was. Thinking it was contraband of some kind, it was confiscated, later to be returned.

The Sinkonnens settled in a northern Minnesota rural community that had strong connections to Scandinavian immigration. They purchased an old Finnish homestead, which included a small house and a few outbuildings, including a sauna (pronounced "sow-na") that housed a wood-burning sauna stove and a dressing room. The Sinkonnens used the sauna every day, including throughout the harsh Minnesota winters. Paavo would often go directly from the heat of the sauna into the snow, rolling in the snow before returning to the sauna for another round of heat.

Paavo worked in a printing company in a nearby city. His work was on the factory production line. He had completed high school in Finland. He was a superb athlete, particularly expert in track and cross-country skiing. If he had stayed in Finland, he would most certainly have been hired as a cross-country skiing coach, a prestigious profession in Finland. Because of his lack of a college education, his employment options in a professional field in the United States were more limited. The leisure activities of the family included running, skiing, gardening and cooking.

The Sinkonnens' two boys were born in the late 1970s and went to a rural school. Paavo and Seija instilled the importance of education into their children. When the oldest child was a senior in high school, he decided that he had not learned everything that he could. Although he was an honors student, he asked and was granted permission to repeat his senior year. During his second senior year, he applied for college to Dartmouth. He was not granted admission, so decided to defer college for a year and reapply to Dartmouth. His second application was successful. During the year after high school, he worked at minimum wage jobs and continued to live at home. During his sophomore year at Dartmouth, his parent received a letter from one of their son's math professors. The professor told Seija and Paavo that their son was an excellent student with an amazing learning ethic. His professor said that their son was one of only a few students he had in his career who exhibited such a tremendous desire and respect for learning, and that he wanted to let them know that they had done an excellent job as parents. Seija and Paavo were proud of their son and humbly shared the letter with a friend who was a professor at a local university. They shared the letter only because they wanted to know if parents' receiving a letter from a professor was a common thing in the United States.

Activity 7.4

Use the preceding example to respond to the following.

1. What parts of the example did you find unusual (and in what ways)?

2. What are the most important values of the Sinkonnen family?

3. What are the most important values in your family?

4. Describe parts of the case study and their relationship to characteristics and systems of culture.

5. For each example of system and characteristic of culture, describe similarities and differences between your culture and the culture described in the case study.

Example: Sense of Distance

When I was teaching at the University of Minnesota in Duluth, one of my students, Jeff, was a graduate student in education. He had grown up on Park Point, a small neighborhood of Duluth that was on a narrow strip of land jutting out into Lake Superior. Park Point was only a few blocks wide and about three miles long, with one side facing an important shipping bay in Superior, Wisconsin, and the other side facing the open lake. Park Point was connected to Duluth by an aerial life bridge. During shipping season, traffic was often backed up on Park Point due to the raising of the bridge to allow 1000-foot freighters to pass from the lake into the bay.

The main city of Duluth is on a steep hill. From Park Point, the lights of the city at night are beautiful. During Jeff's childhood, Park Point was a tightly knit residential community. There was an elementary school, a middle school, a small grocery store, a community center, and a city park at the end of the point. All other services were available across the short bridge in Duluth. Jeff was a middle child in a family with 10 children. His father worked in Duluth and his mother stayed at home with the children. The family was Ojibwe Indian. The family struggled financially with one small income.

Jeff had never been out of the Park Point neighborhood until he went to high school across the bridge. The distance across the short bridge that spanned the narrow shipping canal could have been an ocean. The family did not have a car and public transportation was limited. But it was not the physical distance that prevented them from leaving. Joggers frequently jogged from the mainland side to Park Point. Rather, it was a cultural and status distance that prevented the children from leaving the neighborhood.

When it was time for Jeff to attend high school, he was terrified. Despite his concerns about how he would be treated in the city, he went to the high school. He was not only the first person in his family to go on to graduate from college and graduate school. He was also the first person to graduate from high school.

ACTIVITY 7.5

Use the preceding example to respond to the following.

1. How did you define your own neighborhood as a child?

2. How much did you travel outside of your neighborhood as a child?

3. What parts of the preceding example did you find unusual (and in what ways)?

4. Describe parts of the preceding example and their relationship to characteristics and systems of culture.

5. For each example of system and characteristic of culture, describe similarities and differences between your culture.

ACTIVITY 7.6

1. Using the previous examples as models, write a story about your family. Incorporate as many characteristics and systems as possible.

2. Identify systems or characteristics you used.

Using Media and Popular Culture to Increase Awareness and Understanding of Characteristics and Systems of Culture

Newspapers, magazines and television provide ample opportunity to explore diversity issues at local, national, and global levels. There are a number of steps that can be taken to help you identify and evaluate sources of news that will fit into your lifestyle. Following is a list of steps and a series of activities designed to help you apply the steps to diversity awareness and understanding.

IDENTIFY NEWS SOURCES THAT FIT YOUR LIFESTYLE

Depending on your daily routine, the type and amount of media that are available and convenient to you will vary. Some people subscribe to and read a daily newspaper. Others watch an evening 30-minute national news broadcast or a cable news summary available 24 hours a day. Internet news sources are also widely available.

If your routine is variable and time is limited, a good source of diversity-related news can be found at www.diversityinc.com. This web site gives a weekly summary of diversity-related news in the United States, and provides links to each of several stories.

IDENTIFY THE PERSPECTIVE AND POTENTIAL BIASES OF NEWS SOURCES

The perspective and potential biases of a source are sometimes easy to identify (e.g., the political orientation of talk radio host Rush Limbaugh) and sometimes more difficult (e.g., mainstream news organizations, major newspapers). Sometimes perspectives are more difficult to identify. For example, is an ultrathin female news anchor biased when reporting on obesity in children? A good gauge for identifying objectivity can include how many perspectives on the topic were covered and at what level. The more perspectives that are included, the better.

IDENTIFY THE LEVEL OF THE ANALYSIS OF NEWS SOURCES

How complete the coverage is of an issue is widely variable. A two-minute segment on the national news will generally cover fewer perspectives than longer, more in-depth segments. However, length of time spent may not always reflect multiple perspectives. If a story does not cover the event or issue fully, it is important to think about how the source fits into the big picture of the issue.

EXAMINE THE DETERMINATION OF NEWSWORTHINESS

What does it mean when some news events receive attention and others do not? How does determination of newsworthiness reflect cultural values? For example, India and Pakistan have been fighting over Kashmir for decades. The conflict received increased news attention when it was discovered that both India and Pakistan have nuclear capabilities.

ACTIVITY 7.7

Watch a national television newscast (30-minute minimum). Using the following table, evaluate the newscast for the following concepts.

1. Indicate the source of the newscast, time and date.

2. List all story topics.

3. For each story, indicate whether or not there is a diversity connection. If yes, what is the type of diversity?

4. Indicate whether each story is national or international?

5. What are the characteristics and systems inherent in each story?

6. What other diversity-related concepts are part of each story (e.g., ethnocentrism, stereotyping, dominant privilege)?

Story topic?	Diversity concepts?	Potential Biases of Source?	Systems/ Characteristics?

ACTIVITY **7.7**, CONTINUED

Story topic?	Diversity concepts?	Potential Biases of Source?	Systems/ Characteristics?

ACTIVITY 7.8

Watch or listen to an in-depth (at least 10 minutes) television news segment of a current diversity-related event or issue. In-depth analyses can be found on television on cable news channels, segments on network news magazines, and on public television. National Public Radio is an excellent source for radio news programming.

1. Describe the diversity-related event or issue.

2. Describe the relevance of the story to you.

3. What were the perspectives included in the story?

4. How well do you think the news segment presented multiple perspectives?

5. What characteristics and systems are part of the event or issue?

6. How well did the story present the facts (level of awareness)?

7. How well did the story explore the background and reasons (level of understanding)?

USING POPULAR CULTURE TO INCREASE AWARENESS AND UNDERSTANDING OF DIVERSITY

Popular press magazines, television, music, movies and books all reflect characteristics and systems of culture. Becoming more aware of both (a) what pieces of popular culture you select and (b) the messages and meaning within those pieces is a helpful way to use existing aspects of your life to understand diversity.

ACTIVITY 7.9

1. Visit a magazine stand or magazine section of a store or library.

2. Select five examples of magazines. Choose at least a few that you do not read or that are unfamiliar to you. For each, list the following:

   a. their intended audience

   b. characteristics of the culture of the audience

   c. underlying values and beliefs of the culture

ACTIVITY 7.10

1. Select and watch a movie of your choice.

2. Describe examples of characteristics and systems of culture from the movie. Be as detailed as possible in your analysis.

3. Discuss the underlying values and beliefs in the movie.

Using the Internet for Diversity-Related Information: Challenges and Opportunities

In addition to the media discussed in the previous section, the Internet is an excellent source of information and news about diversity. The Internet is also unique to other more traditional resources because of the massive amount of easily available information. Those characteristics create both challenges and opportunities. Challenges include the proliferation of hate groups and organizations on the Internet, and potential difficulty in identifying the source and credibility of Internet websites. Opportunities include the instant access to up-to-the-minute information, and the amount of information on both specialized and general websites.

PROLIFIERATION OF HATE GROUPS AND ORGANIZATIONS ON THE INTERNET

There are many hate groups and organizations whose messages have proliferated through hundreds of Internet sites and chat rooms. The presence of the Internet sites has led to renewed discussion of the relationship of free speech, hate groups and hate crimes. It has also led to greater membership.

While the Ku Klux Klan is perhaps the most well-known hate group, there are many other groups that have been associated with hate and violence. Neo-Nazi skinheads embrace Nazi ideology and often have gang lifestyles. The Identity Church Movement uses Christianity to support anti-Semitic and racist beliefs. The Nation of Islam, led in the United States by Louis Farrakhan, is anti-Semitic, anti-White, anti-gay and anti-Catholic.

The Southern Poverty Law Center (*www.splcenter.org*) tracks the activities of over 500 hate groups. Other useful sources of information on hate groups include numerous federal government agencies, including the Department of Justice; the Anti-Defamation League (*www.adl.org*); the National Association for the Advancement of Colored People (*www.naacp.org*); the American-Arab Anti-Discrimination Committee (*www.adc.org*); the National Gay & Lesbian Task Force (*www.ngltf.org*) and the Simon Wiesenthal Center (*www.wiesenthal.com*). The Gay and Lesbian Alliance Against Defamation (GLAAD) seeks to eliminate homophobia and discrimination based on gender identity and sexual orientation.

ISSUES OF SOURCE AND CREDIBILITY ON THE INTERNET

Internet technology allows virtually anything to be posted on the Internet by anyone, and then be viewed by potentially millions of people. It is therefore very important when viewing web sites to be aware of the source, perspective and credibility of the information, and to be even more cautious than with traditional media sources.

Web-based design has made it possible and common to deliberately deceive people looking for information. For example, if you log on to *www.whitehouse.org*, you will have accessed what looks like a government site, but is actual-

---

ACTIVITY 7.11

1. Discuss the relationship of free speech and hate groups. Identify as many issues as you can.

2. On the Internet, find and read the mission statement for a hate group.

3. How easy or difficult was it for you to locate a hate group site?

4. List five values from the mission statement that you share.

5. List five values from the mission statement that you do not share.

6. What surprised you about the hate group site? Was it what you expected?

---

ly not. The site uses the same visual format, logo and link categories as the site *www.whitehouse.gov*, the official site of the government. If you go to *www.whitehouse.com*, you will be on what the web site claims to be "Voted the #1 adult site!"

Sometimes web addresses are nearly identical with no deceit intended. For example, *www.Stop-the-Hate.org* and *www.Stop-the-Hate.com* refer to the same site. The site is a good source for information on specific hate groups, and also for general information about world religious perspectives. The address for *www.StopTheHate.org* is very close, but the site is for a group that focuses on tolerance and anti-discrimination resources and efforts in schools.

Strategies for effectively using the Internet for diversity-related information include the following points.

◆ Use search engines that include reviewed websites wherever possible. This will assist you (most of the time, but not always) in separating reputable sources from others. It will also help you to narrow your search if your keyword search yields hundreds or thousands of websites.

◆ Use multiple search engines. Different search engines will often yield different results. Some examples of commonly used search engines are Netscape, Google, Yahoo, Internet Explorer, AltaVista, AskJeeves, Excite, HotBot, Look Smart and Lycos.

◆ Try to document the web addresses of the sources you are finding as you go along. Be sure when you print documents to also write the website address (if it is not printed), so that you can cite the source appropriately and get back to the website if you need additional information. You should also note the date you accessed the information. (If an update date is given, note that also.)

◆ One way to determine the perspective of the source is by using the website address. For example, noting whether the end of the address is .com, .org, .gov or .edu will give you clues about the intent of the site.

◆ Remember that websites change frequently and can be removed entirely, so if you find information you think you will want, download or print it whenever possible.

USEFUL INTERNET SOURCES FOR DIVERSITY-RELATED INFORMATION

Developing an exhaustive list of diversity-related internet websites is beyond the scope of this section. Rather, this section includes a sample of types of sources that provide a variety of types of information, and can be used as a starting point for many diversity topics. (Some of these websites have also been cited elsewhere in this book.)

Diversity-Related Organizations. Many organizations (included those listed earlier in this section) provide information. The site can be about a specific type of diversity or group (e.g., the American-Arab Anti-Discrimination Committee). The site may be about a specific person. For example, the family of Dr. Martin Luther King, Jr., has a website where his speeches and other materials are available.

Some organizations provide information on specific topics. For example, the Southern Poverty Law Center, led by Morris Dees, reports on legal cases and provides resources to educators and community groups, including many links to other sites.

Universities. The University of Maryland diversity website (cited earlier) includes many topics and links related to diversity, including a glossary of diversity terms. The University of Maryland and the American Association of Colleges and Universities sponsor www.diversityweb.org, an excellent site for many higher education resources. Stanford University has an excellent site on the papers of Dr. Martin Luther King, Jr. The University of Colorado has diversity related links on many topics.

University websites developed by instructors and students about specific courses are also common. While many are excellent, a caution in using these sites is to remember that information within the site is not likely to be reviewed or edited in the same way as other sources.

Individuals and Groups. Websites posted by individuals and groups can be wonderful resources for personal accounts. (But once again, keep in mind the caution noted in the previous paragraph.) An example of an individual site is Uncle Donald's Castro Street (*www.thecastro.net*). The site was started several years ago as a personal account of life in the San Francisco gay community in the 1970s. It includes links to Harvey Milk, a San Francisco politician who was murdered on November 27, 1978. (Harvey Milk was chosen by *Time* magazine as one of the 100 most influential people of the 20th century.) One link uses narrative and photographs to show the candlelight march and

tell the story of the grief felt by the residents of San Francisco the night of the murder.

A good source for information about Japanese-American internment camps during World War II is *www.geocities.com/athens/8420/main.html*. The site has many links and includes photographs by Dorothea Lange, a famous photographer of the time. The photographs help to dramatically show the personal tragedy of the internment.

Despite the cautions, there are advantages of using websites by individuals and groups. First, they allow the reader to get a very personal perspective, with some of the elements of oral history. Second, it may be easier and faster to ask questions and get a personal response from the website author than with an organization. For example, in the writing of this book I was trying to find some information about a quote from Harvey Milk. I could not find the answer to my question on the more formal and academic websites or in published sources. I contacted Uncle Donald's Castro Street and received an answer the same day.

News and Information Sources. All of the major television networks have websites. I have found CNN and ABC to be particularly useful. MTV has an ongoing "Fight for Your Rights: Take a Stand Against Discrimination" campaign focusing on hate crimes. Their website link to the campaign includes stories, chat rooms and news updates.

Most major newspapers and magazines also have websites. A free subscription source of diversity-related news designed for business is Diversity Inc (*www.diversityinc.com* was mentioned earlier in this book). Each week several stories related to diversity are profiled; links are provided for additional information. This site is an excellent source for discovering current diversity-related events that might or might not be easily found in other news sources. This site requires a subscription for full stories but a free trial is available.

Government Sources. For employment discrimination, the Equal Employment Opportunity Commission (*www.eeoc.gov*) is the starting point for information. The Department of Justice address is *www.usdoj.gov*.

There are several websites for Americans with Disabilities Act (ADA) information and compliance, including the ADA home page (*www.usdoj.gov/crt/ada/adahom1.htm*), the U.S. Architectural and Transportation Barriers Compliance Board (*www.access-board.gov*) and the Disability and Business Technical Assistance Centers (*www.adata.org*).

Diversity glossaries. Understanding both the basic concepts and the complexities of diversity can be enhanced by an exploration of the many Internet glossary sites available. Go to a search engine and type in the word you are interested in, plus "glossary" and you will generally get several concise and informative sites, often from universities or specific diversity advocacy organizations.

ACTIVITY 7.12

1. Find an Internet diversity glossary site. Include the web address.

2. Select a term that is new and interesting to you. Include the web definition.

3. Describe how the term is related to at least one concept from the course.

Using National and Global Issues and Events to Increase Awareness and Understanding of Characteristics and Systems of Culture

The previous two sections included discussions of the role of media (including news) as a way to explore characteristics and systems of culture. When national and global issues are identified, connections can be made to specific characteristics and systems that are useful in understanding cultural differences. Two ideas for using national and global issues follow: (a) taking a snapshot of current events and (b) in-depth exploration of specific issues or events.

TAKING A SNAPSHOT OF CURRENT EVENTS

Identifying a list of diversity-related current events or issues at any given time serves several purposes. First, a list identifies what types of diversity are in the news (e.g., race, ethnicity, gender). Second, a list can be used to identify the proportion of national and global events that are highlighted. Third, a list can serve as a barometer for public interest in types of events and issues. A good website for current events with topic-based links is from the U.S. Department of the Interior (www.doi.gov/diversity/8current). The following is a list of examples from a "snapshot" during a week in May 2004.

- Photographs showing U.S. soldiers brutalizing Iraqi prisoners were published. New accounts focus on the perpetrators and their training, as well as inquiries about whether the events were isolated or systemic.
- The 50th anniversary of the Brown versus Board of Education legislation has produced multiple news stories from a variety of perspectives, including first person accounts of Black students at the time, questions about the successes and failures of the legislation, and controversy about the display of a Ku Klux Klan robe in the Smithsonian exhibit commemorating the Brown versus the Board of Education decision.
- A bill in Brazil's Congress calls for landowners who use slave labor to have their land confiscated and redistributed to former slave laborers. The bill is in response to Brazilian president Luiz Inacio Lula da Silva's new measures to counter slavery in the country.

ACTIVITY 7.13

1. Develop a snapshot list of diversity-related national and global events and issues in the news.

2. Describe the relevance of the issues to you. Which issues are the most relevant? Which issues are the least relevant?

3. Which of the issues and events are national and which are global? What is the meaning of the proportion?

4. What are the "diversity gaps" in the snapshot list?

5. Select three issues. On each, what are your opinions about the balance of coverage? What is missing? What questions do you have? How would you get more information? How do the issues represent concepts such as ethnocentrism, stereotyping and dominant privilege?

- Police investigating a rape at the University of Virginia, Charlottesville, randomly collected DNA samples from nearly 200 African-American men, who were all cleared as suspects.

- The Justice Department announced it is reopening the murder investigation of Emmett Till, who was murdered in 1955 in Mississippi, and whose death was a catalyst for events in the civil rights movement.

- In Massachusetts, leaders on Cape Cod voted to offer marriage licenses to out-of-state same-sex couples, in opposition to the interpretations of federal and state law of Governor Mitt Romney, who has threatened legal action because of a 1913 state law. On May 17, 2004, gay marriages became legal in Massachusetts.

- Residents of a Florida town are deeply divided about renaming a street in honor of Martin Luther King, Jr.

- A Latino day laborer in Georgia was picked up by a group of men promising work. He was then beaten. Prosecution based on a hate crime is being considered.

- A Northeastern University study that included 366 police departments in Massachusetts found that nearly three-fourths of the departments engaged in racial profiling of drivers of color.

- Since 1995, 19 African American-men have died in confrontations with Cincinnati police officers. Racial tensions in Cincinnati continued with rumors about a death of a Black man, later determined to be a suicide.

- The FBI has stepped up monitoring of hate groups that advocate violence on the Internet. This follows the recent conviction of Matt Hale, a white supremacist and founder of the World Church of the Creator, whose racial hatred was linked to the two murders by a follower of the church.

IN-DEPTH EXPLORATION OF INDIVIDUAL ISSUES OR EVENTS

Identifying the characteristics and systems of culture inherent in current issues and events allows for a more in-depth exploration by helping to isolate important factors. Isolating important factors in turn allows for the development of questions and ideas that can be used to further understand components of culture.

Example: Elian Gonzales

A passing fisherman picked up Elian Gonzales off the coast of Florida on Thanksgiving Day 1999. Elian's mother and several other people drowned during the ill-fated attempt to illegally enter the United States from Cuba. Elian then moved in with Miami, Florida, relatives until it could be determined whether or not he should remain with his Florida relatives or return to Cuba to live with his father.

During the next several months, it was determined by the Immigration and Naturalization Service (INS) that Elian should be returned to Cuba. The Miami relatives challenged the decision in court. Elian's grandmothers visited the United States to plea for their grandson's return to Cuba. In April 2000, Elian's father, stepmother, and infant half-brother arrived in the United States, vowing to not return to Cuba without Elian. In a controversial predawn raid by the INS, Elian was removed from the home of his Miami relatives and returned to his father. Elian and his father returned to Cuba in summer 2000 after further court proceedings.

Hundreds of protesters from the Cuban-American community argued that Elian would have a better quality of life and chance for success in the United States, and should be allowed to stay. Another argument in favor of Elian staying in the United States was that his mother had died trying to gain freedom for herself and her son, and that her wishes should be honored. Influential Cuban-Americans, including singer Gloria Estefan and actor Andy Garcia, became involved in the controversy and concurred.

Proponents of returning Elian to Cuba felt strongly that the boy should be returned to his father in Cuba. The dominance of family over political and socioeconomic issues was considered to be most important. Another argument for returning Elian to Cuba was that it would be more difficult to try to negotiate the return of children with an American parent who had been taken to another country by a non-American parent if Elian Gonzales was not returned to his father. Ultimately, Elian Gonzalez was returned to his father and the family lives in Cuba.

ACTIVITY 7.14

Use the previous example to respond to the following.

1. Why do you think the Elian Gonzales story was so prominent in the news?

2. What stereotypes, ethnocentric perspectives and examples of dominant privilege are in the example?

3. What systems of culture are part of the Elian Gonzales example?

4. What characteristics of culture are part of the Elian Gonzales example?

5. What questions related to cultural values can be created based on the characteristics and systems of culture identified (e.g., relationship of socioeconomic status to quality of life, should income be a criterion to become a parent)?

ACTIVITY 7.15

1. Select an example of a national or global issue or event with a diversity connection.

2. What is your personal interest in the issue or event?

3. Describe the issue or event as fully as you can. You will probably need to do some exploration of the issue or event through newspaper, television, magazine and/or Internet sources.

4. Identify important characteristics and systems of culture connections and discuss each.

5. What questions related to cultural values can be created based on the characteristics and systems of culture identified?

6. How difficult was it to find information on many perspectives in the issue?

Using Cultural Profiles to Increase Understanding of Characteristics and Systems of Culture

Exploring specific cultures can help in understanding characteristics and systems of that culture, and in understanding controversial issues within the culture. The following case study will illustrate that concept by providing a brief background on Deaf culture (including reference to selected characteristics and systems of culture), followed by a discussion of the controversy in the Deaf community surrounding the use of cochlear implants.

The case study is included for two purposes. First, Deaf culture is complex. Learning a little about the culture (and recognizing that the case study cannot fully explore the cultural characteristics) can be a starting point for more learning. Second, the case study can serve as a model for how other cultures can be better understood by examining specific characteristics and systems.

The Deaf Community: A Cultural Profile

Laura J. Kelly, Ph.D.
(printed with permission)

Using Characteristics and Systems of Culture to Understand Deaf Culture

Cultural profiles can be described as aspects of a culture that are the foundation for some of the beliefs, values and behaviors that make the culture distinct. Cultural profiles are not intended to identify all of the important components of a culture nor are they a substitute for personal interaction. They are intended to be an introduction to the complexity of a particular community and to the framework that can be used to understand it.

The following profile of Deaf culture provides an example that can be used to explore the framework of characteristics and systems of culture. Identifying individuals with limited access to sound as a cultural group is controversial outside of the Deaf community. The controversy has arisen because individuals who are deaf are typically viewed from a medical perspective. The medical perspective is a deficit model that treats deafness as a disorder to be cured instead of as a physical difference. The Deaf culture perspective suggests that an individual who is deaf lives in a visual world that includes the use of a visual language. The absence of hearing becomes a barrier only in situations where hearing individuals are unwilling to adapt. It should be noted that the word "deaf' is capitalized when used in the context of Deaf culture when it refers to the individuals who are associated with the community. A lower case "d" is used when referring to the presence of limited hearing. It should also be noted that the context of this discussion is limited to Deaf culture in the United States. The language (oral and signed) and practices of individuals who are deaf varies around the world just as it does with individuals who hear.

Cultural Membership

Individuals who are deaf can be divided into two primary groups, oral communicators and manual communicators. Oral deaf include people who rely on hearing (if any remains), speechreading (lip movements, facial expression and gestures) and spoken language to communicate. Manual communicators use sign language as their method of communication. Individuals who view themselves as oral are not considered members of the Deaf community. The first and most important characteristic of someone in the Deaf community is the use of American Sign Language (ASL) as their primary means of communication. ASL has its own grammar and syntax, and it is not directly translatable to or from English. A number of universities in the United States now accept ASL as a substitute for a foreign language requirement. The Deaf community views ASL as the natural language of the deaf. It is more than a part of their heritage; it is the defining feature of their identity. Other forms of sign language that are based on rules of English are viewed as attempts by the hearing world to "fix" a communication form that is considered by the hearing as inferior and to exert control over the education of individuals who are deaf. The history of deaf education in the United States is filled with stories of hearing teachers in schools using oral instruction methods that required students to sit on their hands to prevent them from using ASL or used rulers to strike the hands of children who persisted in signing. Therefore, in addition to being a language, ASL is a source of Deaf pride and a symbol of the Deaf communities persistence in the face of ignorance within the hearing community.

Education

American Sign Language may be learned from family members in the home; however, since 90% of individuals who are deaf are born to hearing parents, ASL is usually learned via interaction with other deaf individuals. A child's first exposure to ASL and Deaf culture often occurs in school. Schools for the deaf are viewed as having a key role in transmitting cultural identity and helping to maintain a strong community. The choice of the type of school and the communication mode the child will use has a direct impact on the extent to which the child will identify with the Deaf community. Hearing parents may select a school on the basis of many factors including location or access to oral methods of instruction. If deaf parents have a deaf child they often want him or her to attend the same school for the deaf they attended. It is common for deaf parents to be pleased their child is deaf because it means they share a bond with their child that includes a broader understanding of the visual world. Hearing children of deaf parents who sign will learn to sign and eventually become bilingual. These hearing children are accepted into the Deaf community though their status is considered slightly lower than someone who is born deaf.

Additional opportunities for community interaction can occur through groups such as Deaf social clubs, sports clubs, churches and synagogues. While individuals with hearing are not banned from such gatherings, the ability (or at least a willingness) to engage in conversation via sign language is an indication of a hearing individual's level of respect for the culture and its members.

Communication

Because ASL is a visual language, maintaining visual contact with the "speaker" is very important. Looking away from someone who is signing can be interpreted to mean that the "listener" is bored or disinterested. If a hearing person turns to another person and uses oral communication without translating what is being said, the communicator will be viewed as rude, because he or she has excluded the person who uses sign language. Individuals who wish to hold a private conversation will turn their backs to the group and "whisper" by signing close to their bodies in a smaller space. If a professional interpreter is present, eye contact should be maintained with the person who is deaf and conversation should be directed to them and not to the interpreter. Since the interpreter is there to act as a conduit for communication and not a message receiver, he or she is ignored.

Understanding the context of a conversation in ASL is very important. Many signs have meanings that change depending on the context of the conversation. ASL also uses space to denote meaning. When joining a conversation late, it may be necessary to spend some time acclimating to the topic of the conversation in order to gain full understanding of what or who is being discussed. For example, instead of using "he" or "she" the signer might designate a particular point in space to represent the person. From that time on anything signed within that space is attributed to that person. A new arrival to the conversation would need to wait until the person is identified by name again or ask to be filled in at the conclusion of the story.

Like English, ASL is a fluid language. Every day, new signs emerge to meet the needs of the community. Some signs like the Deaf equivalent of clapping (the signer raises both hands and rapidly rotates them at the wrist), spread rapidly and are adopted throughout the Deaf community. At other times, different cities and regions develop variations of a sign and that sign is used within that area. Signs can be developed by a family as well and used exclusively within a household. These are referred to as "home signs." *Multiculturalism*

Privacy

Privacy within the Deaf community is viewed a bit differently than in the hearing community. Because individuals within the community often view each other as family, topics of conversation between members who are not related or who do not have regular contact with one another may seem too personal or too blunt to outsiders. For example, one member might comment to another that they seemed to have gained weight since the last time they saw them. In addition, since members of the community often have to rely on hearing friends or family to interpret for them, personal information may be made available to a wider circle of people than many hearing individuals are accustomed to. Perhaps a reasonable comparison would be the rapid dissemination of information that is often associated with living in a very small town.

Personal Space

A person who is signing needs space to do so. ASL is a three dimensional language and therefore standing too close may interfere with an individual's ability to sign freely. However, physical contact is often necessary. When gaining someone's attention or joining a conversation it is considered polite to tap them on the shoulder or touch them on the arm and wait for a your presence to be acknowledged. Greetings often include hugging before stepping back to provide an adequate space for signing a clear visual field.

Art and Tradition as Cultural Expression

Many people are not aware that American Sign Language does not have a written equivalent. Poetry and stories in ASL are particularly difficult to translate into written English because of their use of three dimensional space as part of the poetic imagery. As a result, the Deaf community has retained traditions of poetry, jokes, story telling and folklore by passing them on to members visually. Jokes in the Deaf community often revolve around the hearing culture. It is not uncommon for hearing characters and hearing customs to be the brunt of the jokes.

An interesting story telling tradition involves the use of the manual alphabet. A word is selected and the storyteller creates a story using the letters in the word as the first letter for each word in the story. In addition, the hand shape of the letters themselves must be incorporated into how the word is signed. Consequently there are three levels of visual imagery—the foundation word, the hand shapes used to create the letters in the foundation word and the signs used for the words in the story.

An outgrowth of the Deaf culture visual arts tradition is The National Theatre of the Deaf. It is an internationally acclaimed group of artists who present original ASL and translated English to ASL works in theatres around the world. (Schirmer, 2001).

Rutherford (as cited in Schirmer 2001) identifies naming as an example of one folkloric tradition. Within the Deaf community, a person being introduced to another for the first time will spell out his or her name and then provide a short version called a "name sign." The name sign often consists of the first letter of the person's name signed in particular space or in a fashion that represents some characteristic of the individual. A name sign is generally not created by the individual, but is used first by a member of the Deaf community. It is a nickname that has meaning only within the context of Deaf culture.

The preceding profile provides an opportunity to gain greater understanding of a unique American community. As noted previously, the extent to which Deaf communities in other parts of the world share the characteristics described here will vary. However, there is no doubt that the use of ASL in the United States acts a binding force and a source of pride for those individuals who are a part of the Deaf community.

A Current Issue in Deaf Culture: Cochlear Implants

Background

The following discussion of a controversial issue in Deaf culture—cochlear implants—provides an opportunity to examine differences in cultural values and how those values impact upon the decision making process of families.

A cochlear implant is an electronic device that stimulates the nerves that carry sound to the brain. It is used in situations where a standard hearing aid does not provide significant benefit. A surgical procedure is performed that involves creating a shallow indentation and electrodes connected to the receiver/transmitter are placed deep within the ear inside the area known as the cochlear and next to the hearing nerves. Using a microphone and a special processing device worn outside the body, sound is coded and transmitted to the receiver/transmitter underneath the skin and transferred to the electrodes. The electrodes generate a series of electrical pulses to stimulate the nerves. When the external device is turned off or disconnected the person cannot hear at all in that ear. The external device is worn during the day and removed at night.

Not all individuals with a hearing loss are candidates for a cochlear implant. The degree of the hearing loss must be severe. The location and type of the damage to the ear must be documented. Obviously, if the hearing nerve is the location of the damage an implant will not work. A child must be at least 18 months old and must have tried other forms of amplification before he or she is considered a candidate. Individuals who agree to the implant must be willing to undergo a period of training in order to learn to recognize the sensations created by the implant. The sensations generated by the implant are different than the sounds a person with hearing experiences or even the sounds heard with the use of a hearing aid. For children, the training includes both listening exercises as well as speech therapy stretching over many years. The level of success achieved with a cochlear implant varies greatly. Some individuals may only be able to detect the presence or absence of sounds while others may be able to hold a conversation on the phone with a stranger. Since telephone conversations are carried out without the help of visual clues (gestures, facial expressions, lip movements) this communication skill is considered an indication of a high level of success. Young children and adults implanted soon after losing their hearing seem to have the best chance of success. It is also important to consider that when the electrodes are threaded into the cochlea this area of the ear is irreparably damaged. Thus, if the implant proves to be unsuccessful the individual would not be able to use other forms of amplification on that ear. For this reason, only one ear is implanted, although research trials are underway in which some adults may elect to receive a second implant if the first one has proven to be successful.

Case Study: Cultural Conflict Within Families

The case is adapted from a documentary film called *Sound and Fury* (2000) that records a few months in the lives of two families as they decide whether to have their children receive cochlear implants. (*Sound and Fury* was nominated for an Academy Award for best documentary.)

Elise and her sister grew up with their brother Mark in New York. Their parents John and Liz began to suspect Elise could not hear when she was about six months old, but since she seemed to respond to some sounds they did not ask their physician about it until she was a year old. The pediatrician clapped behind Elise's back and she turned toward him. The doctor felt that was adequate proof of hearing and told John and Liz that Elise was fine. Eight months later when Elise still had not started talking John and Liz went to an audiologist. Testing confirmed the couple's suspicions that Elise had a profound hearing loss. Her apparent response in the doctor's office had probably been to vibration or to the puff of air generated by the doctor's clap. Elise was fitted with hearing aids and her parents worked hard with her to help her adjust to them. They talked and read to her and did lessons to help her develop speech. Her progress was slow and Elise often became frustrated because she could not communicate her needs. When she entered school she lagged behind the other students despite extra assistance. Her teachers and the other students could not understand her speech. Her parents eventually enrolled her in the Lexington School for the Deaf and started to learn sign language.

As she grew up, Elise began to develop ties with the Deaf community. Her parents did learn some sign language though even now they still expect Elise to use speech reading to understand them when they do not know the sign for something. Elise eventually married George Dillion, a classmate at the Lexington School for the Deaf. After high school, George attended Gallaudet University (a university for the deaf) while Elise worked as a manicurist. They were married immediately after George graduated. Four years after they were married, their daughter Brenda was born. Because both of her parents were deaf, Brenda's hearing was tested soon after birth and it was determined that Brenda was deaf as well. Her parents were delighted. They communicate with Brenda using American Sign Language although she also wears hearing aids. The hearing aids provide her with an awareness of some environmental sounds. Brenda's grandparents were upset to learn that their grandchild was deaf. When Brenda stays with them, Liz works with her as she did with her daughter to try to improve her speech. Liz spends a great deal of time caring for Brenda and talks to Brenda about how exciting it would be for her to hear other children and how she would love to be able to talk to Brenda on the phone.

Brenda has begun to talk about cochlear implants and how much she would like to be able to talk on the phone. At her parents' urging, Elise decided to gain further information. George and Elise visit programs that specialize in teaching children using oral methods of communication. A child who receives a cochlear implant would need to be enrolled in a program where learning speech is a high priority. In one program that George and Elise visit, all the children use speech and do not use ASL. They watch Brenda interact with the other children and note her frustration when she tries to talk to the other children and they do not understand her sign language or when she tries to use the speech she has learned. They also visit a school where instruction is in ASL and see that Brenda seems to fit in right away. Elise is reminded of her own childhood and how frustrated she was when people could not understand her speech and how isolated she felt when she was with hearing children.

Liz and Elise talk about Elise's childhood. Liz says that she does not want her grandchild to experience the same isolation that Elise did. Brenda is already starting to feel left out when she plays with hearing children in the neighborhood. Liz wants her to have a better life than Elise and she believes the cochlear implant will help her achieve it by giving her access to the hearing world. Elise responds that she feels her mother views her as inferior because she cannot speak clearly. Growing up, Elise felt isolated within her own hearing family. Unlike her, Brenda will grow up surrounded by people who speak the same language as she does and will know she is part of a community with shared experience. Elise and George decide not to have Brenda receive the cochlear implant.

Elise's sister, Caroline, is three years younger and is hearing. Caroline learned sign language growing up with her sister and is comfortable interacting with individuals in the Deaf community. Caroline met her husband, Allen, at a party sponsored by the local Deaf Club. He is hearing and his parents are Deaf. Their first daughter, April, was born hearing and a year later Diane was born. Testing revealed Diane was deaf. Caroline and Allen elected to have their child fitted with hearing aids and soon began investigating whether Diane would be a candidate for a cochlear implant. Caroline's parents are enthusiastic about the prospect and encourage Caroline to talk to Elise about an implant for Brenda.

In contrast, Allen's parents, Carl and Barb, are adamantly opposed to Diane receiving a cochlear implant. They express concern that they will be unable to talk to their granddaughter and she will never understand what it is like to be a part of the Deaf community. They stress the implant will not make her hearing and in fact will only confuse her as to her identity. At a picnic sponsored by the local Deaf club, Carl and Barb get into a heated discussion about cochlear implants with Allen and Caroline. Individuals around them are drawn into the discussion. Caroline talks about how she wants the best for her child and feels the cochlear implant will widen her opportunities and give her the chance to live a normal life. Carl and Barb say these comments hurt them deeply. It implies the life they lead is not good enough. They ask, "What is normal? Don't we have jobs and friends?" Caroline says she wants Diane to hear music and be able to hear the birds sing. Barb and Carl say they have never heard these things and therefore they do not miss them. They can feel wind and see beautiful things around them. Sound is not a requirement for a full life and they are proof of that. The people around them agree. They say the cochlear implant is a way for hearing people to destroy the Deaf community and take away the children that can best understand and appreciate a shared experience, language, and history. Despite Carl and Bob's concerns, Caroline and Allen decide to go ahead and proceed with the cochlear implant for Diane.

References

Schirmer, B. (2001). *Psychological, social and educational dimensions of deafness.* Needham Heights, MA: Allyn and Bacon.

Sound and Fury (2000) Aronson Film Associates and Public Policy Productions in Association with Thirteen/ WNET Channel 4.

ACTIVITY 7.16

Use the preceding cultural profile to answer the following questions.

1. What are some characteristics of culture associated with the Deaf culture?

2. Which family in the case study do you empathize the most with and why?

3. What is your opinion of Liz and her interaction with Elise and her family?

4. To what extent should hearing people accommodate the communication needs of the deaf community?

5. To what extent should deaf people accommodate to the communication styles of the hearing world?

6. How does an even greater understanding of Deaf culture affect your opinions about Cochlear implants?

PART III

Application

Using Legislation and Literature to Understand Diversity

"Morality cannot be legislated but behavior can be regulated. Judicial decrees may not change the heart, but they can restrain the heartless."
Dr. Martin Luther King, Jr., *Strength to Love*, 1963

"If we are to achieve a richer culture, rich in contrasting values, we must recognize the whole gamut of human potentialities, and so weave a less arbitrary social fabric, one in which each diverse human gift will find a fitting place."

Margaret Mead

Objectives of Chapter 8

The overall objective of Chapter 8 is to explore the relationship between societal values and beliefs and legislation and literature related to diversity. Specific objectives follow.

❖ Explore examples of legislation, such as Civil Rights Acts, the Americans with Disabilities Act, existing and proposed hate crime legislation, and the United Nations Universal Declaration of Human Rights
❖ Identify pivotal events in the civil rights movements
❖ Identify myths of legislation
❖ Understand the historical context of legislation and political events
❖ Use the Equal Rights Amendment to examine gender issue
❖ Examine the relationship between legislation and societal behavior, attitudes and values
❖ Use selected speeches (e.g., Sojourner Truth, Martin Luther King, the Pledge of Allegiance) to explore diversity issues
❖ Use selected literature and quotes to explore diversity issues

Introduction

Exploring examples of legislation and literature, including important speeches, is a useful way to examine the philosophical and historical perspectives of diversity issues. Several examples from the United States will be included and discussed in this chapter. You are encouraged to use these discussions as a springboard for the analysis of other examples.

There is a rich variety of multicultural literature that is not within the scope of this chapter. Literature about cultures and literature written by people representing various cultural perspectives is widely available. Readers are encouraged to explore such sources.

Legislation Related to Diversity

There is considerable legislation in the United States related to diversity issues. Some examples are related to types of diversity, such as race, age, gender and religion, among others. Other examples relate to specific contexts, such as education, housing and immigration.

The discussion in this section represents a sampling of legislation or amendments proposed or enacted. Examples were selected because of their impact (e.g., the Civil Rights Acts, the Americans with Disabilities Act of 1990) or their political or historical importance (e.g., the Equal Rights Amendment, hate crimes legislation, the United Nations Universal Declaration of Human Rights). All examples are useful in reflecting societal values and challenges.

CIVIL RIGHTS LEGISLATION

There have been several examples of civil rights legislation passed in the United States, including The Civil Rights Acts of 1957, 1960, 1964, 1968, 1983 and 1991. The Civil Rights Act of 1964 represents a response to a series of national events and considerable attention to civil rights. The Civil Rights Act of 1964 prohibited discrimination on the basis of race, color, sex, religion and national origin. In the Civil Rights Act of 1991, disability was added as a protected class.

In addition to prohibiting discrimination on the basis of people in a protected class, civil rights legislation created agencies to educate people about the laws or monitor or enforce the laws. For example, the Civil Rights Act of 1957 established the United States Commission on Civil Rights (USCCR). A new USCCR was established under the Civil Rights Act of 1983. The USCCR is a fact-finding agency of the Executive Branch.

A second example of an agency created by civil rights legislation is the Equal Employment Opportunity Commission (EEOC). The EEOC was established in the Civil Rights Act of 1964. The EEOC investigates complaints of employment discrimination.

The civil rights movement in the 1950s and 1960s involved hundreds of thousands of people in the United States, including many in favor and many opposed to increasing civil rights. Many pivotal events shaped the civil rights movement.

Although these events did not occur in the lifetime of current traditional-age college students, most people in the U.S. over 50 years of age have memories of the events. Younger students are encouraged to talk to older people about that time to get a greater and richer sense of the history. The following example includes a sampling of important civil rights events.

Example: Events of the Civil Rights Movement of the 1950s and 1960s

◆ The "separate but equal" precedent was set in the 1896 Plessy v. Ferguson ruling.

◆ The 1954 Supreme Court Brown v. Board of Education of Topeka, Kansas, ruling overturned Plessy v. Ferguson, banning school segregation.

◆ Emmett Till, a 14-year-old African-American boy from Chicago, is murdered on August 28, 1955 in Mississippi after whistling at a White woman. Two men who later confess to the murder are acquitted by an all-White jury. Publicity and protests around the country follow.

◆ In 1955, Rosa Parks was arrested after refusing to give up her seat near the front of a bus in Montgomery, Alabama. Community leaders, including Dr. Martin Luther King, Jr., organized a bus boycott. Eight months later, the Supreme Court ruled that bus segregation was illegal.

◆ In 1957, the governor of Arkansas ordered National Guardsmen to prevent Black students from entering the newly desegregated Little Rock High School. For three weeks the students could not enter school. A mob of 1,000 townspeople gathered daily to support the segregation. President Eisenhower ordered 11,000 troops to Little Rock and the school was desegregated.

◆ In 1960, a Black college student launched a protest against not being served by sitting daily at the lunch counter of a Woolworth's in Greensboro, North Carolina. National attention about the protest inspired similar protests around the country.

◆ In 1961, the nonviolent protest of "Freedom Rides" involved busloads of people riding cross-country to protest segregation of bus terminals.

◆ In 1962, two students were killed at the University of Mississippi during riots following the arrival of the first Black student on campus.

◆ In 1963, many nonviolent protests were held to protest segregation. One protest march, led by Dr. King, Reverend Abernathy and Reverend Shuttlesworth, led to their arrest. During his incarceration, Dr. King wrote the famous "Letter from the Birmingham Jail."

◆ The "March on Washington" in 1963 included 200,000 civil rights supporters. It was at this event that Dr. King gave his "I Have a Dream" speech.

◆ In 1964, "Freedom Summer" included the training of several hundred civil rights workers in Oxford, Ohio. Shortly after the training, three civil rights workers were murdered.

◆ In 1965, a peaceful demonstration in Selma, Alabama, led to violence by state troopers. Violence against the marchers and residents of a nearby housing project led to the labeling of the event as "Bloody Sunday."

◆ In 1968, Dr. King was in Memphis, Tennessee, to mediate an ongoing garbage strike between Black workers and White employers. He delivered his speech "I've Been to the Mountaintop" on April 3, on the eve of his assassination.

ACTIVITY 8.1

Use the preceding example to respond to the following.

1. Which of the preceding events did you know about?

2. Which of the preceding events did you not know about?

3. Which events were triggered by the efforts of one or a few people?

4. Speculate about how it would feel to be Rosa Parks or the college student at the lunch counter or the child entering the elementary school.

THE AMERICANS WITH DISABILITIES ACT (ADA) OF 1990

Although the ADA is a type of civil rights legislation, it is discussed separately here because of its expansion of civil rights for people with disabilities. The purpose of the ADA is to provide equality for people with disabilities in a variety of areas, including access to public accommodations, public transportation and employment. Disabilities include both physical and mental conditions. Over six million people in the United States are considered to have permanent disabilities.

The ADA is very broad and is enforced on a case-by-case basis. There are two key phrases that are used to determine whether discrimination has occurred—"undue hardship" and "reasonable accommodation." In employment, physical facilities or public transportation, the two phrases are used to assess whether an employer, owner of a business or other public facility or transportation company could reasonably accommodate a person with a disability without undue hardship. For example, if it is determined that it would be too expensive to remodel a small retail store to accommodate customers using wheelchairs, the business would not be expected to make such physical changes. The business would, however, need to have a plan to accommodate customers (e.g., on-line shopping, personal shoppers).

Defining undue hardship and reasonable accommodation is clearly a value-laden process. What is undue hardship? How much money is too much money to make a physical modification to a space? What is reasonable accommodation? What seems reasonable to one person might not seem reasonable to another person. The following activity illustrates some of the complexities of these issues.

ACTIVITY 8.2

1. Describe whether each of the following is a reasonable accommodation in your opinion.

2. For each, discuss why the accommodations are reasonable or unreasonable.

3. In the cases where the accommodations are not reasonable in your opinion, suggest alternatives.

   ◆ A second-floor restaurant trains the busboys to carry a wheelchair up the steps.

   U- what about person- leave 1st for them or get elevator

   ◆ A man with bipolar disorder applies for a job. Because he sometimes needs time off for medical appointments to monitor and adjust his medication, the employer refuses to hire him unless the employee takes a salary cut.

   R- should apply for job that accommodates him

   ◆ A restaurant with an inaccessible front entrance uses the back entrance for patrons with wheelchairs. The back entrance route goes through the kitchen, and enters the dining room through the kitchen doors used by the servers.

   U- unsanitary- should make entrance accessible

   ◆ A campus bookstore has a flight of steps at the only public entrance. The accommodation for people in wheelchairs is to have employees come outside and take the book order from the person who cannot enter the space.

   U- all should be allowed in CAMPUS BS. " "

   ◆ A new campus building that houses a college of design (including interior design, architecture and landscape architecture departments) is not accessible. Although the building was completed in 1995, after the passage and enactment of the Americans with Disabilities Act, the university claims that because the design drawings were approved prior to the ADA, the building does not need to comply.

   ◆ A person with cerebral palsy needs additional time to enter and exit a public bus. The bus driver suggests that the person might want to get a taxi, because the bus route schedule is being disrupted and other passengers are upset.

   ◆ A university with many residence halls has several residence halls that are accessible to people using wheelchairs. Most residence halls are inaccessible, including a residence hall for first-year students that includes programming that focuses on diversity issues.

   ◆ A retail clothing store with inaccessible dressing rooms has a liberal return policy for people using wheelchairs.

ACTIVITY 8.2, CONTINUED

◆ In an auditorium, the last row of seats at the rear is removed for use by people in wheelchairs.

◆ In an auditorium, people using wheelchairs are put in the aisles during performances.

◆ A woman applies for a receptionist position. She is told that because of her facial scarring that occurred during a fire when she was a child, she does not have the "front-office appeal" required for the job. The firm offers her another job with equivalent pay.

ACTIVITY 8.3

1. Develop a class list of issues of why some of the examples in the previous activity were considered to be unreasonable examples (e.g., did not consider the dignity of the person, lack of choice).

2. List ways ideas for accommodation can be developed (e.g., asking people with disabilities).

THE EQUAL RIGHTS AMENDMENT (ERA)

Unlike the various civil rights acts and the ADA legislation discussed previously, the ERA has not been ratified to allow its inclusion as an amendment to the United States Constitution. Historically, the ERA was introduced into every session of Congress between 1923 and 1972. In 1972, it was passed and sent to the states for rat-ification. Thirty-five states have ratified the ERA to date (three short of the necessary 38). Fifteen states remain unratified, including Alabama, Arizona, Arkansas, Florida, Georgia, Illinois, Louisiana, Mississippi, Missouri, Nevada, North Carolina, Oklahoma, South Carolina, Utah and Virginia.

Example: The Equal Rights Amendment

The following is the text of the proposed Equal Rights Amendment

Section 1. Equality of rights under the law shall not be denied or abridged by the United States or by any state on account of sex.

Section 2. The Congress shall have the power to enforce, by appropriate legislation, the provisions of this article.

Section 3. This amendment shall take effect two years after the date of ratification.

ACTIVITY 8.4

1. Were you surprised by the text of the ERA? Why or why not?

2. In your words, what does the ERA say?

3. What are values that suggest support for the ERA?

4. What are values that suggest opposition for the ERA?

5. What questions do you have about the ERA as a political issue?

6. What patterns do you see in looking at which states have ratified the ERA and which states have not?

7. Do you support ratification of the ERA? Why or why not?

8. Do you think the ERA will become a Constitutional Amendment? Why or why not?

HATE CRIME LEGISLATION

Defining and punishing hate crimes is a controversial issue. There are many different definitions of hate crimes. Hate crimes are defined in the federal 1994 Hate Crimes Sentencing Enhancement Act as ". . . crimes in which the defendant intentionally selects a victim, or in the case of a property crime, the property that is the object of the crime, because of the actual or perceived race, color, religion, national origin, ethnicity, gender, disability or sexual orientation of any person." The Hate Crime Statistics Act of 1990 defines hate crimes as ". . . crimes that manifest evidence of prejudice based on race, religion, sexual orientation, or ethnicity, including where appropriate the crimes of murder, non-negligent manslaughter, forcible rape, aggravated assault, simple assault, intimidation, arson, and destruction, damage or vandalism of property."

Issues in hate crime legislation include whether hate crime legislation is or is not necessary, what groups should be included (e.g., religion, sexual orientation, race), how hate crimes are proven, and how punishment should be changed in hate crime cases, among others. Twenty-two states (plus the District of Columbia) have hate crime laws that include sexual orientation. Twenty states have hate crime laws that exclude sexual orientation. Eight states (Arkansas, Georgia, Hawaii, Indiana, Kansas, New Mexico, South Carolina and Wyoming) do not have hate crime laws. A brief description of existing federal laws and proposed legislation follows.

◆ Section 245 of Title 18 of the United States Code permits prosecution when the crime occurred when the victim was participating in a federally protected activity (e.g., voting). Protected classes include race, color, religion and national origin.

◆ The Hate Crimes Statistics Act of 1990 established guidelines for collecting data related to hate crimes.

ACTIVITY 8.5

1. What are your initial opinions about hate crime legislation?

2. Read the Hate Crimes Prevention Act of 1999 (widely available on the Internet).

3. Find and read three Internet sources in favor of expanded hate crimes legislation. What are the sources of the information (e.g., federal government, Southern Poverty Law Center, Anti-Defamation League)? Several web site addresses are listed later in this section.

4. Find and read at least three Internet sources against expanded hate crimes legislation. What are the sources of the information (e.g., specific hate groups)?

5. List the perspectives both for and against hate crime legislation.

6. How do the legislation and the reading you have done support, oppose or change your opinion about hate crime legislation?

◆ The Hate Crime Sentencing Enhancement Act of 1994 was part of a major federal crime bill, and allowed for increasing sentences for crimes that are proven to be hate crimes. This law applies only to crimes committed on federal property. Protected classes include race, color, religion, national origin, sexual orientation, gender and disability.

◆ The Church Arson Prevention Act of 1996 was passed in response to a rash of church arsons.

◆ In 1999, the federal Hate Crimes Prevention Act was introduced and passed by the Senate, but has not yet passed the House of Representatives. The Hate Crimes Prevention Act would broaden existing legislation by removing restrictions on the context of the activity and also expand protected classes to include gender, sexual orientation and disability.

THE UNITED NATIONS UNIVERSAL DECLARATION OF HUMAN RIGHTS

The United Nations Universal Declaration of Human Rights includes 30 articles. The declaration was adopted in 1948, reflecting the idealized shared values of the post-World War II period. The text of the Declaration is included on the following pages.

ACTIVITY 8.6

1. Read the United Nations Universal Declaration of Human Rights.

2. Select one article from the declaration.

3. Describe the values that are inherent in the article you selected.

4. Describe and discuss examples in the United States of issues or events related to the concept of the article. Include issues and events that both support and violate the article.

5. Describe and discuss global examples of issues or events related to the concept of the article. Include issues and events that both support and violate the article.

Universal Declaration of Human Rights
Adopted and proclaimed by General Assembly resolution 217 A (III) of 10 December 1948

Preamble

Whereas recognition of the inherent dignity and of the equal and inalienable rights of all members of the human family is the foundation of freedom, justice and peace in the world,

Whereas disregard and contempt for human rights have resulted in barbarous acts which have outraged the conscience of mankind, and the advent of a world in which human beings shall enjoy freedom of speech and belief and freedom from fear and want has been proclaimed as the highest aspiration of the common people,

Whereas it is essential, if man is not to be compelled to have recourse, as a last resort, to rebellion against tyranny and oppression, that human rights should be protected by the rule of law,

Whereas it is essential to promote the development of friendly relations between nations,

Whereas the peoples of the United Nations have in the Charter reaffirmed their faith in fundamental human rights, in the dignity and worth of the human person and in the equal rights of men and women and have determined to promote social progress and better standards of life in larger freedom,

Whereas Member States have pledged themselves to achieve, in cooperation with the United Nations, the promotion of universal respect for and observance of human rights and fundamental freedoms,

Whereas a common understanding of these rights and freedoms is of the greatest importance for the full realization of this pledge,

Now, therefore,
The General Assembly,

Proclaims this Universal Declaration of Human Rights as a common standard of achievement for all peoples and all nations, to the end that every individual and every organ of society, keeping this Declaration constantly in mind, shall strive by teaching and education to promote respect for these rights and freedoms and by progressive measures, national and international, to secure their universal and effective recognition and observance, both among the peoples of Member States themselves and among the peoples of territories under their jurisdiction.

Article I

All human beings are born free and equal in dignity and rights. They are endowed with reason and conscience and should act towards one another in a spirit of brotherhood.

-/-/-/-/-/-

Article 2

Everyone is entitled to all the rights and freedoms set forth in this Declaration, without distinction of any kind, such as race, colour, sex, language, religion, political or other opinion, national or social origin, property, birth or other status.

Furthermore, no distinction shall be made on the basis of the political, jurisdictional or international status of the country or territory to which a person belongs, whether it be independent, trust, non-self-governing or under any other limitation of sovereignty.

-/-/-/-/-/-

Article 3

Everyone has the right to life, liberty and security of person.

-/-/-/-/-/-

Article 4

No one shall be held in slavery or servitude; slavery and the slave trade shall be prohibited in all their forms.

-/-/-/-/-/-

Article 5

No one shall be subjected to torture or to cruel, inhuman or degrading treatment or punishment.

-/-/-/-/-/-

Article 6

Everyone has the right to recognition everywhere as a person before the law.

-/-/-/-/-/-

Article 7

All are equal before the law and are entitled without any discrimination to equal protection of the law. All are entitled to equal protection against any discrimination in violation of this Declaration and against any incitement to such discrimination.

-/-/-/-/-/-

Article 8

Everyone has the right to an effective remedy by the competent national tribunals for acts violating the fundamental rights granted him by the constitution or by law.

-/-/-/-/-/-

Article 9

No one shall be subjected to arbitrary arrest, detention or exile.

-/-/-/-/-/-

Article 10

Everyone is entitled in full equality to a fair and public hearing by an independent and impartial tribunal, in the determination of his rights and obligations and of any criminal charge against him.

-/-/-/-/-/-

Article 11

1. Everyone charged with a penal offence has the right to be presumed innocent until proved guilty according to law in a public trial at which he has had all the guarantees necessary for his defence.
2. No one shall be held guilty of any penal offence on account of any act or omission which did not constitute a penal offence, under national or international law, at the time when it was committed. Nor shall a heavier penalty be imposed than the one that was applicable at the time the penal offence was committed.

-/-/-/-/-/-

Article 12

No one shall be subjected to arbitrary interference with his privacy, family, home or correspondence, nor to attacks upon his honour and reputation. Everyone has the right to the protection of the law against such interference or attacks.

-/-/-/-/-/-

Article 13

1. Everyone has the right to freedom of movement and residence within the borders of each State.
2. Everyone has the right to leave any country, including his own, and to return to his country.

-/-/-/-/-/-

Article 14

1. Everyone has the right to seek and to enjoy in other countries asylum from persecution.
2. This right may not be invoked in the case of prosecutions genuinely arising from non-political crimes or from acts contrary to the purposes and principles of the United Nations.

-/-/-/-/-/-

Article 15

1. Everyone has the right to a nationality.
2. No one shall be arbitrarily deprived of his nationality nor denied the right to change his nationality.

-/-/-/-/-/-

Article 16

1. Men and women of full age, without any limitation due to race, nationality or religion, have the right to marry and to found a family. They are entitled to equal rights as to marriage, during marriage and at its dissolution.
2. Marriage shall be entered into only with the free and full consent of the intending spouses.
3. The family is the natural and fundamental group unit of society and is entitled to protection by society and the State.

-/-/-/-/-/-

Article 17

1. Everyone has the right to own property alone as well as in association with others.
2. No one shall be arbitrarily deprived of his property.

-/-/-/-/-/-

Article 18

Everyone has the right to freedom of thought, conscience and religion; this right includes freedom to change his religion or belief, and freedom, either alone or in community with others and in public or private, to manifest his religion or belief in teaching, practice, worship and observance.
-/-/-/-/-/-

Article 19

Everyone has the right to freedom of opinion and expression; this right includes freedom to hold opinions without interference and to seek, receive and impart information and ideas through any media and regardless of frontiers.
-/-/-/-/-/-

Article 20

1. Everyone has the right to freedom of peaceful assembly and association.
2. No one may be compelled to belong to an association.
-/-/-/-/-/-

Article 21

1. Everyone has the right to take part in the government of his country, directly or through freely chosen representatives.
2. Everyone has the right to equal access to public service in his country.
3. The will of the people shall be the basis of the authority of government; this will shall be expressed in periodic and genuine elections which shall be by universal and equal suffrage and shall be held by secret vote or by equivalent free voting procedures.
-/-/-/-/-/-

Article 22

Everyone, as a member of society, has the right to social security and is entitled to realization, through national effort and international co-operation and in accordance with the organization and resources of each State, of the economic, social and cultural rights indispensable for his dignity and the free development of his personality.
-/-/-/-/-/-

Article 23

1. Everyone has the right to work, to free choice of employment, to just and favourable conditions of work and to protection against unemployment.
2. Everyone, without any discrimination, has the right to equal pay for equal work.
3. Everyone who works has the right to just and favourable remuneration ensuring for himself and his family an existence worthy of human dignity, and supplemented, if necessary, by other means of social protection. ·
4. Everyone has the right to form and to join trade unions for the protection of his interests.
-/-/-/-/-/-

Article 24

Everyone has the right to rest and leisure, including reasonable limitation of working hours and periodic holidays with pay.
-/-/-/-/-/-

Article 25

1. Everyone has the right to a standard of living adequate for the health and well-being of himself and of his family, including food, clothing, housing and medical care and necessary social services, and the right to security in the event of unemployment, sickness, disability, widowhood, old age or other lack of livelihood in circumstances beyond his control.
2. Motherhood and childhood are entitled to special care and assistance. All children, whether born in or out of wedlock, shall enjoy the same social protection.

-/-/-/-/-/-

Article 26

1. Everyone has the right to education. Education shall be free, at least in the elementary and fundamental stages. Elementary education shall be compulsory. Technical and professional education shall be made generally available and higher education shall be equally accessible to all on the basis of merit.
2. Education shall be directed to the full development of the human personality and to the strengthening of respect for human rights and fundamental freedoms. It shall promote understanding, tolerance and friendship among all nations, racial or religious groups, and shall further the activities of the United Nations for the maintenance of peace.
3. Parents have a prior right to choose the kind of education that shall be given to their children.

-/-/-/-/-/-

Article 27

1. Everyone has the right freely to participate in the cultural life of the community, to enjoy the arts and to share in scientific advancement and its benefits.
2. Everyone has the right to the protection of the moral and material interests resulting from any scientific, literary or artistic production or which he is the author.

-/-/-/-/-/-

Article 28

Everyone is entitled to a social and international order in which the rights and freedoms set forth in this Declaration can be fully realized.

-/-/-/-/-/-

Article 29

1. Everyone has duties to the community in which alone the free and full development of his personality is possible.
2. In the exercise of his rights and freedoms, everyone shall be subject only to such limitations as are determined by law solely for the purpose of securing due recognition and respect for the rights and freedoms of others and of meeting the just requirements of morality, public order and the general welfare in a democratic society.
3. These rights and freedoms may in no case be exercised contrary to the purposes and principles of the United Nations.

-/-/-/-/-/-

Article 30

Nothing in this Declaration may be interpreted as implying for any State, group or person any right to engage in any activity or to perform any act aimed at the destruction of any of the rights and freedoms set forth herein.

ACTIVITY 8.7

1. What societal values and beliefs are reflected in each of the examples from this section?

   a. Civil Rights Acts

   b. Americans with Disabilities Act

   c. Equal Rights Amendments

   d. Federal hate crime legislation

   e. United Nations Declaration of Human Rights

2. How did the societal values and beliefs enhance or hinder passage or ratification?

3. How important are actions of individuals in affecting societal values and beliefs?

Myths about Discrimination Legislation

MYTH 1: LEGISLATION PROVIDES PROTECTION TO EVERYONE AGAINST DISCRIMINATION

As discussed briefly in Chapter 1, discrimination itself is not illegal. Some groups (e.g., homosexuals) are rarely legally protected. Further, legally protected classes are usually specifically defined. For example, if you are over 40 years of age, you can claim age discrimination. However, if you are a college student who is denied an apartment because "we don't rent to college kids," you are not likely to be protected, even though you were discriminated against on the basis of your age.

There are also exemptions in discrimination legislation. For example, in the ADA, small companies with less than a certain number of employees are exempted from some provisions. Also, the physical facilities access provisions do not apply to private housing. So, if you use a wheelchair, for example, a builder, realtor or landlord is not required to modify the space for your needs.

Also, protection against even illegal discrimination is not automatic. If a murder occurs, for example, there is an automatic investigation and charges when a suspect is identified. In discrimination, on the other hand, litigation usually requires action by the victim to trigger an investigation. Not everyone has the time, money or personality to withstand the litigation necessary to legally fight discrimination.

MYTH 2: LEGISLATION HAS ELIMINATED DISCRIMINATION

Legislation has not eliminated discrimination, in part because of the points raised in Myth 1. Also, it is difficult to legislate behavior, whether it is intentional or unintentional bias. In some cases, people find new and subtler ways to discriminate. In other cases (perhaps most cases), people who discriminate do not believe that they discriminate.

While legislation is a crucial element in reducing patterns of discrimination, particularly in the most obvious cases, legislation alone is not enough. There is a critical relationship between the belief systems and behaviors of people and the law. There are many past and present examples of how belief systems and laws have intersected. Sometimes laws lag behind changes in belief systems. In other cases, belief systems have lagged behind the laws.

MYTH 3: DISCRIMINATION IS EASY TO PROVE

This myth is based on the erroneous assumptions that discrimination is both dichotomous and always visible. There are many layers to discrimination and bias, and there are an infinite number of possible manifestations that can be very subtle or very blatant.

ACTIVITY 8.8

1. Think of other myths to add to those described above.

2. Using the three myths included above and those you added, describe examples from current events and issues that reflect the concepts of the myths.

Using Speeches, Quotes and Other Literature to Build Awareness, Understanding and Application of Diversity Concepts

This section includes several examples of speeches, literature and quotes that are useful in understanding diversity. The selected examples have explicit connections and provide a useful starting point. However, it should be noted that everything that one reads can help develop skills in understanding diversity from a broad point of view.

"AIN'T I A WOMAN" SPEECH

Sojourner Truth was an emancipated slave who was active in both anti-slavery and woman's rights movements in the 1800s. The "Ain't I a Woman" speech was given by Sojourner Truth at a women's rights convention in Ohio in 1851. The account of the speech included in this book is from an account recorded by Frances Gage, the president of the convention. The speech is a classic example of the relationship between multiple diversities—in this case, race and gender.

ACTIVITY 8.9

1. Read "Ain't I a Woman."

2. What is your first reaction to the speech?

3. Describe how issues of gender and race are examined in the speech.

4. What characteristics and systems of culture are included in the speech?

Ain't I a Woman?

Several ministers attended the second day of the Woman's Rights Convention, and were not shy in voicing their opinion of man's superiority over women. One claimed "superior intellect," one spoke of the "manhood of Christ," and still another referred to the "sin of our first mother."

Suddenly, Sojourner Truth rose from her seat in the corner of the church.

"For God's sake, Mrs. Gage, *don't* let her speak!" half a dozen women whispered loudly, fearing that their cause would be mixed up with Abolition.

Sojourner walked to the podium and slowly took off her sunbonnet. Her six-foot frame towered over the audience. She began to speak in her deep, resonant voice. "Well, children, where there is so much racket, there must be something out of kilter. I think between the Negroes of the South and the women of the North—all talking about rights—the white men will be in a fix pretty soon. But what's all this talking about?"

Soujourner pointed to one of the ministers. "That man over there says that women need to be helped into carriages, and lifted over ditches, and to have the best place everywhere. Nobody helps *me* any best place. *And ain't I a woman?*"

Sojourner raised herself to her full height. "Look at me! Look at my arm." She bared her right arm and flexed her powerful muscles. "I have plowed, I have planted and I have gathered into barns. And no man could head me. *And ain't I a woman?*"

"I could work as much, and eat as much as man—when I could get it—and bear the lash as well! *And ain't I a woman?* I have borne children and seen most of them sold into slavery, and when I cried out with a mother's grief, none but Jesus heard me. *And ain't I a woman?*"

The women in the audience began to cheer wildly.

She pointed to another minister. "He talks about this thing in the head. What's that they call it?"

"Intellect," whispered a woman nearby.

"That's it, honey. What's intellect got to do with women's rights or black folks' rights? If my cup won't hold but a pint and yours holds a quart, wouldn't you be mean not to let me have my little half-measure full?"

"That little man in black there! He says women can't have as much rights as men. Cause Christ wasn't a woman." She stood with outstretched arms and eyes of fire. "Where did your Christ come from?"

"Where did your Christ come from?" she thundered again. "From God and a Woman! Man had nothing to do with him!"

The entire church now roared with deafening applause.

"If the first woman God ever made was strong enough to turn the world upside down all alone, these women together ought to be able to turn it back and get it right-side up again. And now that they are asking to do it the men better let them."

THE PLEDGE OF ALLEGIANCE

Many children in the United States memorize and recite the Pledge of Allegiance throughout their school years. A recent court case challenged the use of "under God" as a violation of church and state. The Pledge was written in 1892 by Francis Bellamy. It was both published in a leading family magazine and used by a public school program in a flag raising ceremony later that year, thus beginning its popularity.

The text of the original Pledge follows. "I pledge allegiance to my Flag and to the Republic for which it stands, one nation, indivisible, with liberty and justice for all." Bellamy considered the word "equality" but did not include it because of resistance to equality for women and African Americans. In 1924 "my Flag" was changed to "the Flag of the United States of America." In 1954, Congress added the words "under God."

The Pledge illustrates the cultural and historical contexts our documents represent.

"Equality" was not included because there was not support for equality for all. It was not the intent of the author to have a religious tone to the Pledge, despite the fact that he was a Baptist minister. The phrase "one nation, indivisible" was in reference to the Civil War. "One nation, indivisible" today might have an entirely different meaning for a Native American Indian child whose cultural identify is as part of a sovereign nation living within the United States.

THE SPEECHES OF DR. MARTIN LUTHER KING, JR.

In the sampling of civil rights movement events included earlier in this chapter, three of Dr. King's speeches were cited. As a leader of the civil rights movement and as an important historical figure, Dr. King's speeches are insightful in understanding (a) the culture of the 1960s civil rights movement; (b) issues affecting many present-day African Americans; (c) the philosophy of many current civil rights, anti-hate and

ACTIVITY 8.10

1. Select one of Martin Luther King's three speeches mentioned earlier ("Letter from Birmingham City Jail," "I Have a Dream" or "I Have Been to the Mountaintop"). The Martin Luther King, Jr. Papers Project at Stanford University is an excellent source for both his work (e.g., speeches, sermons) and secondary analyses of his work. The web site address is *www.stanford.edu/group/king/*

2. Select a quote from the speech you chose.

3. What is the meaning of the quote you selected?

4. What diversity-related issues are in the quote (e.g., privilege, oppression)?

5. Using the context of the whole speech, what are the societal values that are included in the speech?

6. What other characteristics and systems of culture are integrated into the speech?

7. Are the societal values incorporated into the speech the same for Black and White Americans or different? Discuss your response.

8. Using the context of the speech, discuss (a) what is better now than in the 1960s, (b) what is the same now as in the 1960s and (c) what is worse now than in the 1960s.

anti-discrimination movements and (d) shared values of White and Black Americans.

QUOTES

Quotes are often powerful reflections of values and beliefs. They are also useful in analyzing the meaning and depth of those values and beliefs. The following two activities are designed to increase understanding of diversity using quotes. The first activity uses a self-selected quote to explore both personal and societal values. The second activity uses several examples of quotes that represent diversity concepts (e.g., dominant privilege) that may be more difficult to understand and interpret for some people.

ACTIVITY 8.11

1. Pick one of your favorite quotes or a quote from the beginning of one of the chapters in this book.

2. Describe the personal meaning of the quote to you.

3. Describe the values and beliefs that are represented in the quote.

ACTIVITY 8.12

Discuss the meaning for you of each of the following quotes.

1. "If a bullet should enter my brain, let that bullet open every closet door in America." (This quote is from Harvey Milk, a San Francisco openly gay politician who was murdered in 1978 by another politician. The quote begins one of three audiotapes Milk prepared to be used in the event of his death.)

2. "The most certain test by which we judge whether a country is really free is the amount of security enjoyed by minorities." (Lord Acton, "The History of Freedom in Antiquity," 1907)

3. "To be a Jew is destiny." (Vicki Baum, "And Life Goes On," 1932)

4. "It is better to ask some of the questions than to know all of the answers." (James Thurber, "The Scottie Who Knew Too Much" in "The Thurber Carnival," 1945)

5. "In the new code of laws, remember the ladies and do not put such unlimited power into the hands of the husbands." (A letter from Abigail Adams to her husband, John, in March 1776)

   "I cannot but laugh. Depend upon it, we know better than to repeal our masculine systems." (The letter from John Adams in reply to the letter from his wife Abigail, April 1776)

6. "Words are a form of action, capable of influencing change." (Ingrid Bengis)

BOOKS AND SHORT STORIES

Short stories, books and other literature can be used to identify prevailing cultural values and attitudes, as well as identify other characteristics and systems of culture. The following activities provide a sampling of examples showing how literature can be used to enhance diversity awareness and understanding.

A cautionary note when reading books and short stories is to remember that fiction may or may not represent widespread cultural values of a group. Fiction is usually based on experience or research. It can be an accurate representation of reality or it can be partially or completely made up. Generalizing about a group based on the experiences of specific characters or situations in fiction may be entirely inaccurate.

ACTIVITY 8.13

1. Select a favorite children's book, nursery rhyme or fairy tale.

2. Why is your selection a favorite for you?

3. Develop a list of types of diversity (e.g., race, ethnicity, gender, religion). For each type of diversity, describe the values and beliefs that are inherent in the example of literature you selected.

4. Describe what groups of readers would feel included in the book. What groups of readers would not feel included in the book?

ACTIVITY 8.14

1. Read "A Letter to Harvey Milk" by Lesléa Newman.

2. Using the characteristics and systems of culture framework described in Chapters 5 through 7 of this book, list as many as you can of the following that are included in the story: (a) systems of culture, (b) characteristics of culture and (c) types of diversity.

3. Select and describe the importance in the story of (a) one system of culture (e.g., religion), (b) one characteristic of culture (e.g., leisure, food and eating patterns) and (c) one type of diversity (e.g., sexual orientation, age). Use details and examples to support your descriptions.

A Letter to Harvey Milk

I.

The teacher says we should write about our life, everything that happened today. So *nu*, what's there to tell? Why should today be different than any other day? May 5, 1986. I get up, I have myself a coffee, a little cottage cheese, half an English muffin. I get dressed. I straighten up the house a little, nobody should drop by and see I'm such a slob. I go down to the Senior Center and see what's doing. I play a little cards. I have some lunch, a bagel with cheese. I read a sign in the cafeteria. Writing Class 2:00. I think to myself, why not, something to pass the time. So at two o'clock I go in. The teacher says we should write about our life.

Listen, I want to say to this teacher, I. B. Singer I'm not. You think anybody cares what I did all day? Even my own children, may they live and be well, don't call. You think the whole world is waiting to see what Harry Weinberg had for breakfast?

The teacher is young and nice. She says everybody has something important to say. Yeah, sure, when you're young you believe things like that. She has short brown hair and big eyes, a nice figure, *zaftig* like my poor Fannie, may she rest in peace. She's wearing a Star of David around her neck, hanging from a purple string, that's nice. She gave us all notebooks and told us we're gonna write something every day, and if we want we can even write at home. Who'd a thunk it, me—Harry Weinberg, seventy-seven-years old—scribbling in a notebook like a schoolgirl. Why not, it passes the time.

So after the class I go to the store. I pick myself up a little orange juice, a few bagels, a nice piece of chicken. I shouldn't starve to death. I go up, I put on the slippers, I eat the chicken, I watch a little TV, I write in this notebook, I get ready for bed. *Nu*, for this somebody should give me a Pulitzer Prize?

II.

Today the teacher tells us something about herself. She's a Jew, this we know from the *Mogen Dovid* she wears around her neck. She tells us she wants to collect stories from old Jewish people, to preserve our history. *Oy*, such stories that I could tell her, shouldn't be preserved by nobody. She tells us she's learning Yiddish. For what, I wonder. I can't figure this teacher out. She's young, she's pretty, she shouldn't be with the old people so much. I wonder is she married. She doesn't wear a ring. Her grandparents won't tell her stories, she says, and she's worried that the Jews her age won't know nothing about the culture, about life in the *shtetls*. Believe me, life in the *shtetl* is nothing worth knowing about. Hunger and more hunger. Better off we're here in America, the past is past.

Then she gives us our homework, the homework we write in the class, it's a little *meshugeh*, but alright. She wants us to write a letter to somebody from our past, somebody who's no longer with us. She reads us a letter a child wrote to Abraham Lincoln, like an example. Right away I see everybody's getting nervous. So I raise my hand. "Teacher," I say, "you can tell me maybe how to address such a letter? There's a few things I've wanted to ask my wife for a long time." Everybody laughs. Then they start to write.

I sit for a few minutes, thinking about Fannie, thinking about my sister Frieda, my mother, my father, may they all rest in peace. But it's the strangest thing, the one I really want to write to is Harvey.

Dear Harvey:

You had to go get yourself killed for being a faygeleh? You couldn't let somebody else have such a great honor? Alright, alright, so you liked the boys, I wasn't wild about the idea. But I got used to it. I never said you wasn't welcome in my house, did I?

Lesléa Newman, from *A Letter to Harvey Milk*, Firebrand Books, Ithaca, New York. Copyright © 1988 by Lesléa Newman.

Nu, Harvey, you couldn't leave well enough alone? You had your own camera store, your own business, what's bad? You couldn't keep still about the boys, you weren't satisfied until the whole world knew? Harvey Milk, with the big ears and the big ideas, had to go make himself something, a big politician. I know, I know, I said, "Harvey, make something of yourself, don't be an old shmegeggie like me, Harry the butcher." So now I'm eating my words, and they stick like a chicken bone in my old throat.

It's a rotten world, Harvey, and rottener still without you in it. You know what happened to that momzer, Dan White? They let him out of jail, and he goes and kills himself so nobody else would have the pleasure. Now you know me, Harvey, I'm not a violent man. But this was too much, even for me. In the old country, I saw things you shouldn't know from things you couldn't imagine one person could do to another. But here in America, a man climbs through the window, kills the Mayor of San Francisco, kills Harvey Milk and a couple years later he's walking around on the street? This I never thought I'd see in my whole life. But from a country that kills the Rosenbergs, I should expect something different?

Harvey, you should be glad you weren't around for the trial. I read about it in the papers. The lawyer, that son of a bitch, said Dan White ate too many Twinkies the night before he killed you, so his brain wasn't working right. Twinkies, nu, I ask you. My kids ate Twinkies when they were little, did they grow up to be murderers, God forbid? And now, do they take the Twinkies down from the shelf, somebody else shouldn't go a little crazy, climb through a window, and shoot somebody? No, they leave them right there next to the cupcakes and the donuts, to torture me every time I go to the store to pick up a few things, I shouldn't starve to death.

Harvey, I think I'm losing my mind. You know what I do now every week? Every week I go to the store, I buy a bag of jelly beans for you, you should have something to nash on, I remember what a sweet tooth you have. I put them in a jar on the table, in case you should come in with another crazy petition for me to sign. Sometimes I think you're gonna just walk through my door and tell me it was another meshugeh publicity stunt.

Harvey, now I'm gonna tell you something. The night you died the whole city of San Francisco cried for you. Thirty thousand people marched in the street, I saw it on TV. Me, I didn't go down. I'm an old man, I don't walk so good, they said there might be riots. But no, there were no riots. Just people walking in the street, quiet, each one with a candle, until the street looked like the sky all lit up with a million stars. Old people, young people, Black people, White people, Chinese people. You name it, they were there. I remember thinking, Harvey must be so proud, and then I remembered you were dead and such a lump rose in my throat, like a grapefruit it was, and then the tears ran down my face like rain. Can you imagine, Harvey, an old man like me, sitting alone in his apartment, crying and carrying on like a baby? But it's the God's truth. Never did I carry on so in all my life.

And then all of a sudden I got mad. I yelled at the people on TV: for getting shot you made him into such a hero? You couldn't march for him when he was alive, he couldn't shep a little naches?

But nu, what good does getting mad do, it only makes my pressure go up. So I took myself a pill, calmed myself down.

Then they made speeches for you, Harvey. The same people who called you a shmuck when you were alive, now you were dead, they were calling you a mensh. You were a mensh, Harvey, a mensh with a heart of gold. You were too good for this rotten world. They just weren't ready for you.

Oy Harveleh, alav ha-shalom, Harry

III.

Today the teacher asks me to stay for a few minutes after class. Oy, what did I do wrong now, I wonder. Maybe she didn't like my letter to Harvey? Who knows?

After the class she comes and sits down next to me. She's wearing purple pants and a white T-shirt. "*Feh,*" I can just hear Fannie say, "God forbid she should wear a skirt? Show off her figure a little? The girls today dressing like boys and the boys dressing like girls—this I don't understand."

"Mr. Weinberg," The teacher says.

"Call me Harry," I says.

"O.K., Harry," she says "I really liked your letter you wrote to Harvey Milk. It was terrific, really. It meant a lot to me. It even made me cry."

I can't even believe my own ears. My letter to Harvey Milk made the teacher cry?

"You see, Harry," she says. "I'm gay, too. And there aren't many Jewish people your age that are so open-minded. At least that I know. So your letter gave me lots of hope. In fact, I was wondering if you'd consider publishing it."

Publishing my letter? Again I couldn't believe my own ears. Who would want to read a letter from Harry Weinberg to Harvey Milk? No, I tell her. I'm too old for fame and glory. I like the writing class, it passes the time. But what I write is my own business. The teacher looks sad for a moment, like a cloud passes over her eyes. Then she says, "Tell me about Harvey Milk. How did you meet him? What was he like?" *Nu*, Harvey, you were a pain in the ass when you were alive, you're still a pain the ass now that you're dead. Everybody wants to hear about Harvey.

So I tell her. I tell her how I came into the camera shop one day with a roll of film from when I went to visit the grandchildren. How we started talking, and I said, "Milk, that's not such a common name. Are you related to the Milks in Woodmere?" And so we found out we were practically neighbors forty years ago, when the children were young, before we moved out here. Gracie was almost the same age as Harvey, a couple years older, maybe, but they went to different schools. Still, Harvey leans across the counter and gives me such a hug, like I'm his own father.

I tell her more about Harvey, how he didn't believe there was a good *Kosher* butcher in San Francisco, how he came to my store just to see. But all the time I'm talking I'm thinking to myself, no, it can't be true. Such a gorgeous girl like this goes with the girls, not with the boys? Such a *shana*. Didn't God in His wisdom make a girl a girl and a boy a boy—boom they should meet, boom they should get married, boom they should have babies, and that's the way it is? Harvey I loved like my own son, but this I never could understand. And *nu*, why was the teacher telling me this, it's my business who she sleeps with? She has some sadness in her eyes, this teacher. Believe me I've known such sadness in my life, I can recognize it a hundred miles away. Maybe she's lonely. Maybe after class one day I'll take her out for a coffee, we'll talk a little bit, I'll find out.

IV.

It's 3:00 in the morning, I can't sleep. So *nu*, here I am with this crazy notebook. Who am I kidding, maybe I think I'm Yizhak Perez? What would the children think, to see their old father sitting up in his bathrobe with a cup of tea, scribbling in his notebook? *Oy meyn kinder*, they should only live and be well and call their old father once in a while.

Fannie used to keep up with them. She could be such a *nudge*, my Fannie. "What's the matter, you're too good to call your old mother once in a while?" she'd yell into the phone. Then there'd be a pause. "Busy-shmusy," she'd yell even louder. "Was I too busy to change your diapers? Was I too busy to put food into your mouth?" *Oy*, I haven't got the strength, but Fannie could she yell and carry on.

You know sometimes, in the middle of the night, I'll reach across the bed for Fannie's hand. Without even thinking, like my hand got a mind of its own, it creeps across the bed, looking for Fannie's hand. After all this time, fourteen years she's been dead, but still, a man gets used to a few things. Forty-two years, the body doesn't forget. And my little *Faigl* had such hands, little *hentelehs*, tiny like a child's. But strong. Strong from kneading *challah*, from scrubbing clothes, from rubbing the children's backs to put them to sleep. My Fannie, she was so ashamed from those hands. After thirty-five years of marriage when finally, I could afford to buy her a diamond ring, she said no. She said it was too late already, she'd be ashamed. A girl needs nice hands to show off a diamond, her hands were already ruined, better yet buy a new stove.

Ruined? *Feh*. To me her hands were beautiful. Small, with veins running through them like rivers, and cracks in the skin like the desert. A hundred times I've kicked myself for not buying Fannie that ring.

V.

Today in the writing class the teacher read my notebook. Then she says I should make a poem about Fannie. "A poem," I says to her, "now Shakespeare you want I should be?" She says I have a good eye for detail. I says to her, "Excuse me, Teacher, you live with a woman for forty-two years, you start to notice a few things."

She helps me. We do it together, we write a poem called "Fannie's Hands":

Fannie's hands are too little birds that fly into her lap.
Her veins are like rivers.
Her skin is cracked like the desert.
Her strong little hands
baked challah, scrubbed clothes,
rubbed the children's backs.
Her strong little hands and my big clumsy hands
fit together in the night
like pieces of a jigsaw puzzle
made in Heaven, by God.

So *nu*, who says you can't teach an old dog new tricks? I read it to the class and such a fuss they made. "A regular Romeo," one of them says. "If only my husband, may he live and be well, would write such a poem for me," says another. I wish Fannie was still alive, I could read it to her. Even the teacher was happy, I could tell, but still, there was a ring of sadness around her eyes.

After the class I waited till everybody left, they shouldn't get the wrong idea, and I asked the teacher would she like to go get a coffee, "*Nu*, it's enough writing already," I said. "Come, let's have a little treat."

So we take a walk, it's a nice day. We find a diner, nothing fancy, but clean and quiet. I try to buy her a piece of cake, a sandwich maybe, but no, all she wants is coffee.

So we sit and talk a little. She wants to know about my childhood in the old country, she wants to know about the boat ride to America, she wants to know did my parents speak Yiddish to me when I was growing up. "Harry," she says to me, "when I hear old people talking Yiddish, it's like a love letter blowing in the wind. I try to run after them, and sometimes I catch a phrase that makes me cry or a word that makes me laugh. Even if I don't understand, it always touches my heart."

Oy, this teacher has some strange ideas. "Why do you want to speak Jewish?" I ask her. "Here in America, everybody speaks English. You don't need it. What's done is done, what's past is past. You shouldn't go with the old people so much. You should go out, make friends, have a good time. You got some troubles you want to talk about? Maybe I shouldn't pry," I say, "but you shouldn't look so sad, a young girl like you. When you're old you got plenty to be sad. You shouldn't think about the old days so much, let the dead rest in peace. What's done is done."

I took a swallow of my coffee, to calm down my nerves. I was getting a little too excited.

"Harry, listen to me," the teacher says. "I'm thirty years old and no one in my family will talk to me because I'm gay. It's all Harvey Milk's fault. He made such an impression on me. You know, when he died, what he said, 'If a bullet enters my brain, let that bullet destroy every closet door.' So when he died, I came out to everyone—the people at work, my parents. I felt it was my duty, so the Dan Whites of the world wouldn't be able to get away with it. I mean, if every single gay person came out—just think of it!—everyone would see they had a gay friend or a gay brother or a gay cousin or a gay teacher. Then they couldn't say things like 'Those gays should be shot.' Because they'd be saying you should shoot my neighbor or my sister or my daughter's best friend."

I never saw the teacher get so excited before. Maybe a politician she should be. She reminded me a little bit of Harvey.

"So *nu*, what's the problem?" I ask.

"The problem is my parents," she says with a sigh, and such a sigh I never heard from a young person before. "My parents haven't spoken to me since I told them I was gay. 'How could you do this to us?' they said. I wasn't doing anything to them. I tried to explain I couldn't help being gay, like I couldn't help being a Jew, but that they didn't want to hear. So I haven't spoken to them in eight years."

"Eight years, *Gottenyu*," I say to her. This I never heard of in my whole life. A father and a mother cut off their own daughter like that. Better they should cut off their own hand. I thought about Gracie, a perfect daughter she's not, but your child is your child. When she married the Goy, Fannie threatened to put her head in the oven, but she got over it. Not to see your own daughter for eight years, and such a smart, gorgeous girl, such a good teacher, what a *shana*.

So what can I do, I ask. Does she want me to talk to them, a letter maybe I could write. Does she want I should adopt her, the hell with them, I make a little joke. She smiles "Just talking to you makes me feel better," she says. So *nu*, now I'm Harry the social worker. She says that's why she wants the old people's stories so much, she doesn't know nothing from her own family history. She wants to know about her own people, maybe write a book. But it's hard to get the people to talk to her, she says, she doesn't understand.

"Listen, Teacher," I tell her. "These old people have stories you shouldn't know from. What's there to tell? Hunger and more hunger. Suffering and more suffering. I buried my sister over twenty years ago, my mother, my father—all dead. You think I could just start talking about them like I just saw them yesterday? You think I don't think about them every day? Right here I keep them." I say, pointing to my heart. "I try to forget them, I should live in peace, the dead are gone. Talking about them won't bring them back. You want stories, go talk to somebody else. I ain't got no stories."

I sat down then, I didn't even know I was standing up, I got so excited. Everybody in the diner was looking at me, a crazy man shouting at a young girl.

Oy, and now the teacher was crying. "I'm sorry," I says to her. "You want another coffee?"

"No thanks, Harry," she says, "I'm sorry, too."

"Forget it. We can just pretend it never happened," I say, and then we go.

VI.

All this crazy writing has shaken me up inside a little bit. Yesterday I was walking home from the diner, I thought I saw Harvey walking in front of me. No, it can't be, I says to myself, and my heart started to pound so, I got afraid I shouldn't drop dead in the street from a heart attack. But then the man turned around it wasn't Harvey. It didn't ever look like him at all.

I got myself upstairs and took myself a pill, I could feel my pressure was going up. All this talk about the past—Fannie, Harvey, Frieda, my mother, my father—what good does it do? This teacher and her crazy ideas. Did I ever ask my mother, my father, what their childhood was like? What nonsense. Better I shouldn't know.

So today is Saturday, no writing class, but still I'm writing in this crazy notebook. I ask myself, Harry, what can I do to make you feel a little better? And I answer myself, make me a nice chicken soup.

You think an old man like me can't make chicken soup? Let me tell you, on all the holidays it was Harry that made the soup. Every *Pesach* it was Harry skimming the *shmaltz* from the top of the pot, it was Harry making the *kreplach*. I ask you, where is it written that a man shouldn't know from chicken soup?

So I take myself down to the store, I buy myself a nice chicken, some carrots, some celery, some parsley—onions I already got, parsnips I can do without. I'm afraid I shouldn't have a heart attack *shlepping* all that food up in the steps, but thank God, I make it alright.

I put up the pot with water, throw everything in one-two-three, and soon the whole house smells from chicken soup.

I remember the time Harvey came to visit and there I was with my apron on, skimming the *shmaltz* from the soup. Did he kid me about that! The only way I could get him to keep still was to invite him to dinner. "Listen, Harvey," I says to him. "Whether you're a man or a woman, it doesn't matter. You gotta learn to cook. When you're old, nobody cares. Nobody will do for you. You gotta learn to do for yourself."

"I won't live past fifty, Har," he says, smearing a piece of rye bread with *shmaltz*.

"Nobody wants to grow old, believe me, I know," I says to him, "But listen, it's not so terrible. What's the alternative. Nobody wants to die young, either." I take off my apron and sit down with him.

"No, I mean it Harry," he says to me with his mouth full. "I won't make it to fifty. I've always known it. I'm a politician. A gay politician. Someone's gonna take a pot shot at me. It's a risk you gotta take."

The way he said it, I tell you, a chill ran down my back like I never felt before. He was forty-seven at the time, just a year before he died.

VII.

Today after the writing class, the teacher tells us she's going away for two days. Everyone makes a big fuss, the class they like so much already. She tells us she's sorry, something came up she has to do. She says we can come have class without her, the room will be open, we can read to each other what we write in our notebooks. Someone asks her what we should write about.

"Write me a letter," she says. "Write a story called 'What I Never Told Anyone.'"

So, after everyone leaves, I ask her does she want to go out, have a coffee, but she says no, she has to go home and pack

I tell her wherever she's going she should have a good time.

"Thanks, Harry," she says. "You'll be here when I get back?"

"Sure," I tell her. "I like this crazy writing. It passes the time."

She swings a big black bookbag onto bar shoulder, a regular Hercules this teacher is, and she smiles at me. "I gotta run, Harry. Have a good week." She turns and walks away and something on her bookbag catches my eye. A big shiny pin that spells out her name all fancy-shmancy in rhinestones: Barbara. And under that, right away I see sewn onto her bookbag an upside-down pink triangle.

I stop in my tracks, stunned. No, it can't be, I says to myself. Maybe it's just a design? Maybe she doesn't know from this? My heart is beating fast now, I know I should go home, take myself a pill, my pressure, I can feel it going up.

But I just stand there. And then I get mad, What, she thinks maybe I'm blind as well as old. I can't see what's right in front of my nose? Or maybe we don't remember such things? What right does she have to walk in here with that, that thing on her bag, to remind us of what we been through? Haven't we seen enough?

Stories she wants. She wants we should cut our hearts open and give her stories so she could write a book. Well, alright, now I'll tell her a story.

This is what I never told anyone. One day, maybe seven, eight years ago—no, maybe longer, I think Harvey was still alive—one day Izzie, come knocking on my door. I open the door and, there's Izzie standing there, his face white as a sheet. I bring him inside, I make him a coffee. "Izzie, what is it," I says to him. "Something happened to the children, to the grandchildren, God forbid?"

He sits down, he doesn't drink his coffee. He looks through me like I'm not even there. Then he says, "Harry, I'm walking down the street, you know I had a little lunch at the Center, and then I come outside, I see a young man, maybe twenty-five, a good-looking guy, walking toward me. He's wearing black pants, a white shirt, and on his shirt he's got a pink triangle."

"So," I says. "A pink triangle, a purple triangle, they wear all kinds of crazy things these days."

"*Heshel*," he tells me, "don't you understand? The gays are wearing pink triangles just like the war, just like in the camps."

No, this I can't believe. Why would they do a thing like that? But if Izzie says it, it must be true. Who would make up such a thing?

"He looked a little bit like *Yussl*," Izzie says, and then he begins to cry, and such a cry like I never heard. Like a baby he was, with the tears streaming down his cheeks and his shoulders shaking with great big sobs. Such moans and groans I never heard from a grown man in all my life. I thought maybe he was gonna have a heart attack the way he was carrying on. I didn't know what to do. I was afraid the neighbors would hear, they shouldn't call the police, such sounds he was making. Fifty-eight years old he was, but he looked like a little boy sitting there, sniffling. And who was *Yussl*. Thirty years we'd been friends, and I never head from *Yussl*.

So finally, I put my arms around him, and I held him. I didn't know what else to do. His body was shaking so, I thought his bones would crack from knocking against each other. Soon his body got quiet, but then all of a sudden his mouth got noisy.

"Listen, *Hershel*, I got to tell you something, something I never told nobody in my whole life. I was young in the camps, nineteen, maybe twenty when they took us away." The words poured from his mouth like a flood "*Yussl* was my best friend in the camps. Already I saw my mother, my father, my Hannah marched off to the ovens. *Yussl* was the only one I had to hold on to.

"One morning, during the selection, they pointed me to the right, *Yussl* to the left. I went a little crazy, I ran after him. 'No, he stays with me, they made a mistake,' I said, and I grabbed him by the hand and dragged him back in line. Why the guard didn't kill us right then, I couldn't tell you. Nothing made sense in that place.

"*Yussl* and I slept together on a wooden bench. That night I couldn't sleep. It happened pretty often in that place. I would close my eyes and see such things that would make me scream in the night, and for that I could get shot. I don't know what was worse, asleep or awake. All I saw was suffering.

"On this night, *Yussl* was awake, too. He didn't move a muscle, but I could tell. Finally he said my name, just a whisper, but something broke in me and I began to cry. He put his arms around me and we cried together, such a close call we'd had.

"And then he began to kiss me. 'You saved my life,' he whispered, and he kissed my eyes, my cheeks, my lips. And Harry, I kissed him back. Harry, I never told nobody this before. I, we . . . we, you know, that was such a place that hell, I couldn't help it. The warmth of his body was just too much for me and Hannah was dead already and we would soon be dead too, probably, so what did it matter?"

He looked up at me then, the tears streaming from his eyes. "It's O.K., Izzie," I said. "Maybe I would have done the same."

"There's more, Harry," he says, and I got him a tissue, he should blow his nose. What more could there be?

"This went on for a couple of months maybe, just every once in a while when we couldn't sleep. He'd whisper my name and I'd answer with his, and then we'd, you know, we'd touch each other. We were very, very quiet, but who knows, maybe some other boys in the barracks were doing the same.

"To this day I don't know how it happened, but somehow someone found out, One day *Yussl* didn't come back to the barracks at night. I went almost crazy, you can imagine, all the things that went through my mind, the things they might have done to him, those lousy Nazis. I looked everywhere, I asked everyone, three days he was gone. And then on the third day, they lined us up after supper and there they had *Yussl*. I almost collapsed on the ground when I saw him. They had him on his knees with his hands tied behind his back. His face was swollen so, you couldn't even see his eyes. His clothes were stained with blood. And on his uniform they had sewn a pink triangle, big, twice the size of our yellow stars.

"Oy, did they beat but good. 'Who's your friend?' they yelled at him. 'Tell us and we'll let you live.' But no, he wouldn't tell. He knew they were lying, he knew they'd kill us both. They asked him again and again. 'Who's your friend? Tell us which one he is.' And every time he said no, they'd crack him with a whip until the blood ran from him like a river. Such a sight he was, like I've never seen. How he remained conscious I'll never know."

"Everything inside me was broken after that. I wanted to run to his side, but I didn't dare, so afraid I was. At one point he looked at me, right in the eye as though he was saying, *Izzie, save yourself. Me, I'm finished, but you, you got a chance to live through this and tell the world our story.*

Right after he looked at me, he collapsed, and they shot him, Harry, right there in front of us. Even after he was dead they kicked him in the head a little bit. They left his body out there for two days, as a warning to us. They whipped us all that night, and from then on we had to sleep with all the lights on and with our hands on top of the blankets. Anyone caught with their hands under the blankets would be shot

"He died for me, Harry, they killed him for that, was it such a terrible thing? Oy, I haven't thought about *Yussl* for twenty-five years maybe, but when I saw that kid on the street today, it was too much." And then he started crying again, and he clung to me like a child.

So what could I do? I was afraid he shouldn't have a heart attack, maybe he was having a nervous breakdown, maybe I should get the doctor. *Vay iss mir*, I never saw anybody so upset in my whole life. And such a story, *Gottenyu*.

"Izzie, come lie down," I says, and I took him by the hand to the bed. I laid him down, I took off his shoes, and still he was crying. So what could I do? I lay down with him, I held him tight. I told him he was safe, he was in America. I don't know what else I said, I don't think he heard me, still he kept crying.

I stroked his head, I held him tight. "Izzie, it's alright," I said. "Izzie, Izzie, *Izzaleh*." I said his name over and over, like a lullaby, until his crying got quiet. He said my name once softly, *Heshel*, or maybe he said *Yussl*, I don't remember, but thank God he finally fell asleep. I tried to get up from the bed, but Izzie held onto me tight. So what could I do? Izzie was my friend for thirty years, for him I would do anything. So I held him all night long, and he slept like a baby.

And this is what I never told nobody, not even Harvey. That there in that bed, where Fannie and I slept together for forty-two years, me and Izzie spent the night. Me, I didn't sleep a wink, such a lump in my throat I had, like the night Harvey died.

Izzie passed on a couple months after that. I saw him a few more times, and he seemed different somehow. How, I couldn't say. We never talked about that night. But now that he had told someone his deepest secret, he was ready to go, he could die in peace. Maybe now that I told, I can die in peace, too?

VIII.

Dear Teacher:

You said write what you never told nobody, and write you a letter. I always did all my homework, such a student I was. So *nu*, I got to tell you something. I can't write in this notebook no more, I can't come no more to the class. I don't want you should take offense, you're a good teacher and a nice girl. But me, I'm an old man, I don't sleep so good at night, these stories are like a knife in my heart. Harvey, Fannie, Izzie, *Yussl*, my father, my mother, let them all rest in peace. The dead are gone. Better to live for today.

What good does remembering do, it doesn't bring back the dead. Let them rest in peace.

But Teacher, I want you should have my notebook. It doesn't have nice stories in it, no love letters, no happy endings for a nice girl like you. A bestseller it ain't. I guarantee. Maybe you'll put it in a book someday, the world shouldn't forget.

Meanwhile, good luck to you, Teacher. May you live and be well and not get shot in the head like poor Harvey, may he rest in peace. Maybe someday we'll go out, have a coffee again, who knows? But me, I'm too old for this crazy writing. I remember too much, the pen is like a knife twisting in my heart.

One more thing, Teacher. Between parents and children, it's not so easy. Believe me, I know. Don't give up on them. One father, one mother, it's all you got. If you were my *tochter*, I'd be proud of you.

Harry

GLOSSARY OF YIDDISH TERMS

challah: yeast-leavened, white egg-bread traditionally eaten on ceremonial occassions, like the Sabbath (Shabbat)

gottenyu: Oh God! (anguish)

kreplach: small pockets of dough filled with meat, like ravioli or wonton; slang for nothing, something valueless

mensh: positive term describing a man with respect; also mentsh or mensch

meshugeh: crazy

meyn kinder: my children

momzer: little wild kid, no goodnik (with affection or with distaste)

naches: pleasures

nu: so? well?

nudge: pushy person

Pesach: Passover

shana: beautiful, pretty

shlep: to carry, to lug

shmaltz: grease or fat

shmegeggie: old fogie, old man

shtetls: Jewish neighborhoods, usually poor and segregated, in eastern european cities and towns during the seventeenth, eighteenth, nineteenth and twentieth centuries.

tochter: daughter

zaftig: voluptuous, soft, sexy

Strategies for Diversity Challenges

"We will remember not the words of our enemies, but the silence of our friends."

Reverend Dr. Martin Luther King, Jr.

"A lot of people think they have to be big dogs to make a difference. That's not true. You just need to be a flea for justice. Enough committed fleas biting strategically can make even the biggest dog uncomfortable."

Sojourner Truth, in Marian Wright Edelman,
***The Measure of Our Success*, 1992**

Objectives of Chapter 9

The overall objective of Chapter 9 is to explore personal strategies you can use for continued diversity awareness, understanding and application. Specific objectives follow.

❖ Develop an understanding of personal perceptions of types of diversity
❖ Explore specific diversity-related strategies for speaking out
❖ Develop specific diversity-related strategies for more genuine and effective communication
❖ Understand the challenges and barriers to using higher level critical-thinking skills in diversity communication
❖ Explore the explicit and implicit diversity messages in college and university web sites and promotional information
❖ Evaluate the culture of institutions such as colleges or universities
❖ Critique the meaning of institutional diversity strategies in a college or university

As we have seen in previous chapters, the process of exploring diversity includes raising awareness of diversity-related issues and developing ways to critically examine those issues. After levels of awareness and understanding are raised, the challenge becomes how to synthesize and apply new information and new ways of thinking to many situations. This chapter explores strategies to meet that challenge.

Developing Personal Strategies for Diversity Issues

Strategies for dealing with diversity are very personal. Each person's response to diversity-related challenges will be different. What is offensive or hurtful to one person may be acceptable to another. What one person feels is important to respond to another may not. The key to developing personal strategies for diversity issues is to evaluate the importance of an issue to you and your comfort level for various responses to diversity-related situations.

ASSESSING YOUR PERSONAL FEELINGS ABOUT TYPES OF DIVERSITY

The following activities are designed to help you identify your own level of response to various types of diversity interactions and observations. What you learn from these activities will

---

ACTIVITY 9.1

1. Describe the biggest diversity challenges in your personal life.

2. Describe what you anticipate will be the biggest diversity challenges in your professional life.

3. What types of diversity did you include in the previous questions? What types of diversity were not included?

ACTIVITY 9.2

1. Develop an "I will" list that reflects what you are comfortable doing. (Example: "I will try to get information on as many sides of an issue as I can before making a decision about how I feel.")

2. For each "I will" statement, describe the personal barriers or challenges to doing it. (Examples: "It is hard for me to ask people their opinions." "It is hard to make the effort to get information on all sides of an issue when I believe what I believe is right.")

3. For each barrier or challenge, describe a way you can reduce it. (Example: "I will make an effort to identify one belief I have and ask someone with a different opinion why they think the way that they do." "I will identify ways that being aware of different opinions can help me think about things more completely.")

ACTIVITY 9.3 TYPES OF DIVERSITY

1. Make a list of types of diversity (e.g., socio-economic status, sexual orientation, disability, religion).

2. Rank order those that interest or are important to you, with "1" being the highest.

3. For those that are highly ranked, make a list for each of the reasons why it is important to you. (Examples: You are part of the nondominant group in that type of diversity or you feel you will need a greater awareness of the type of diversity in your professional life.)

4. For those that are lower ranked, make a list for each of the reasons why it is less important to you. (Examples: You feel it is not important, not a value, disagree, etc.)

5. Examine the reasons you have given in the previous two questions (a) to explore your underlying values and beliefs, (b) to identify patterns in your thinking and (c) to evaluate the meaning of those patterns in your awareness and understanding of diversity.

6. In what ways do your values and beliefs enhance or hinder your diversity strategies?

help you to develop specific diversity-related strategies that will incorporate your individual beliefs and personality.

DEVELOPING SPECIFIC DIVERSITY-RELATED STRATEGIES FOR SPEAKING OUT

The success you have in developing specific diversity-related strategies is dependent on how well the strategies incorporate your individual beliefs and personality. Deciding when to speak up and what to say when you observe someone saying something that is insensitive or hurtful is a common challenge. In addition to being a personal decision and based on your personality and comfort level, what you decide to do is also contextual. What you do in one situation may be different than in another situation. The following activities and examples are included to help you (a) explore your feelings about common situations and (b) develop strategies for dealing with diversity situations.

ACTIVITY 9.4

1. For each type of diversity listed (religion, sexual orientation, disability, socio-economic status, gender, race and ethnicity), specify a particular category (e.g., for disability, someone who uses a wheelchair or someone with bipolar disorder). For each type of diversity, describe your comfort level in the following situations.

	Category	Comfort Level with Diversity	Comfort Level by Situation
Initiating a conversation with someone who is . . .			
Religion (Specify)			
Sexual orientation (Specify)			
Disability (Specify)			
Socio-economic status (Specify)			
Gender (Specify)			
Race (Specify)			
Ethnicity (Specify)			
Having a roommate who is . . .			
Religion (Specify)			
Sexual orientation (Specify)			
Disability (Specify)			
Socio-economic status (Specify)			
Gender (Specify)			
Race (Specify)			
Ethnicity (Specify)			

ACTIVITY 9.4, CONTINUED

	Category	Comfort Level with Diversity	Comfort Level by Situation
Working closely in a job with someone who is . . .			
Religion (Specify)			
Sexual orientation (Specify)			
Disability (Specify)			
Socio-economic status (Specify)			
Gender (Specify)			
Race (Specify)			
Ethnicity (Specify)			
Marrying someone who is . . .			
Religion (Specify)			
Sexual orientation (Specify)			
Disability (Specify)			
Socio-economic status (Specify)			
Gender (Specify)			
Race (Specify)			
Ethnicity (Specify)			

2. Discuss the differences in your comfort level by type of diversity.

3. Discuss the differences in your comfort level by type of situation.

ACTIVITY 9.5

1. Describe what you could do in the following situations.

   ◆ Your friend refers to a student athlete as "a stupid jock."

   ◆ Your boss describes bargaining for a car as "Jewing down" the salesperson.

   ◆ Your friend jokingly calls another friend a "fag."

   ◆ A family member refers to a low-income single-parent mother (who works a full-time minimum wage job) in your neighborhood as "lazy and stupid."

   ◆ A good friend tells a sexist joke.

   ◆ (If you are not African American) Your grandmother refers to her African American neighbors as "the colored people."
     (If you are African American) Your grandmother refers to her White neighbors as "Crackers."

   ◆ A good friend tells a joke about gays.

ACTIVITY **9.5**, CONTINUED

- ◆ Your friend describes someone he or she does not like as a "fag."

- ◆ Your male professor consistently glances at the breasts of women who ask questions in class.

- ◆ A good friend tells a racist joke.

2. For each of the preceding examples, indicate what factors you considered in your response (e.g., the level of importance of the issue was to you, the age of the person, the relationship of the person to you).

3. What are some other examples of when peer or family behavior made you uncomfortable?

4. What is your typical reaction style in new and unfamiliar situations (e.g., sit back and watch, jump right in)?

5. How do you think your reaction style affects your responses in the previous situations?

ACTIVITY 9.6

1. Assume you have talked to someone about an offensive or hurtful comment. Consider what you might do in situations where a person responds to you in the following ways.

   ◆ "Terms change so much I never know what is OK to call people. I can't keep up."

   ◆ "There wasn't anyone here who cared or was offended."

   ◆ "It was just a joke. It didn't mean anything. It was just funny."

   ◆ "People are just too sensitive."

   ◆ "Political correctness has gone too far."

   ◆ "Talking about diversity just makes the problem worse."

ACTIVITY 9.6, CONTINUED

◆   "If we just respect everyone, there will be no problem."

◆   "The problem is groups like the Ku Klux Klan—most people don't have prejudices and biases."

◆   "If people were just educated there would be no problem. People who are educated don't have prejudices and biases."

2. For each of the previous responses, what is underlying emotion (e.g., defensiveness, fear)?

3. Why do you think people become defensive, fearful, etc. when they are questioned about a diversity-related challenge?

4. Add other statements that you have heard to the list in the first question.

There are several reasons why it is important for people in the dominant culture in whatever type of diversity (e.g., gender, sexual orientation, race) to speak out when offensive or hurtful comments or language are used about others. The following is a sample of those reasons.

- Silence implies agreement.
- Silence suggests the issue is important only for those people in the nondominant group.
- Silence sends a message to children and, as part of their socialization, is part of what creates systemic societal bias.

Examples: Challenges to Speaking Out

Example #1

I was the only female on a committee where a graduate student was presenting work on his thesis. In both the written and oral work, the male student consistently referred to school principals as "he," teachers as "she" and students as "he." When I commented on the language, his response was "I would not have done it if I had known a woman was going to be here." None of the White males said anything to the student. My comment became a "woman's issue" and the teachable moment was lost.

Example #2

At a large first-year orientation session for new students and their parents, a parent asks a residence life staff member "Does my child have to keep a roommate of another race if one is assigned?" The staff member is unsure how to respond.

Example #3

A Jewish student is pledging a fraternity. Part of the initiation ceremony involves pledging allegiance to Jesus Christ. The student refuses. The fraternity members and other pledges are unsure what to do.

ACTIVITY 9.7

Use the preceding examples to respond to the following.

1. What would you have done in each of the preceding examples?

2. What are the possible responses of the people involved in each of the examples?

3. What are the possible benefits of each response you have identified?

4. What are the possible risks of each response you have identified?

5. Think of at least one additional example of a challenging situation.

6. What are the possible responses for your example?

7. What are the risks and benefits for your example?

DEVELOPING SPECIFIC DIVERSITY-RELATED STRATEGIES FOR MORE EFFECTIVE COMMUNICATION

Speaking out against offensive, hurtful, biased or prejudiced language, comments and policies is an essential, but not sufficient element for diversity strategies. Understanding the underlying fears and barriers to genuine communication must complement the development of strategies for speaking out explored in the previous section. The following example and activity explore that concept.

Example: Challenges to Effective Diversity Communication

In a class of 25 students, there is one Black student. During a class discussion, the issue of race is brought up. Many White students glance at the Black student. She points out to the White student sitting next to her that he looks at her whenever race is mentioned. His response is that he didn't—his eyes just twitched. (Note: This action is called "totalizing"—making one speak for the whole.)

ACTIVITY 9.8

Use the preceding example to respond to the following.

1. What is your initial reaction to the example?

2. What do you think the Black student was feeling?

3. What do you think the White student was feeling?

4. Why do you think each student said what he or she did to the other student?

5. How might the situation have been altered to improve communication?

6. Describe fears and barriers to communication for those in the dominant group (e.g., being called a racist, offending someone, looking uninformed).

7. Describe fears and barriers to communication for those in the nondominant group (e.g., offending, appearing overly sensitive or "militant," personal safety).

8. Discuss the differences and similarities in the fears and barriers for dominant and nondominant groups.

ACTIVITY 9.9

1. Report (or create) an example of an awkward diversity-related situation.

2. Describe what you think the most common responses would be.

3. Explore why the most common response occurs.

4. Develop some effective responses that could be applied to the example you reported or created.

CHALLENGES AND BARRIERS TO USING HIGHER LEVEL CRITICAL-THINKING SKILLS IN DIVERSITY COMMUNICATION

Previous chapters of this book have focused on developing skills in increasing diversity awareness and understanding. Exploring multiple perspectives and identifying underlying values and assumptions have been central concepts in developing higher level critical-thinking skills. Questioning as a form of information gathering has been stressed.

In communicating with others, questioning and exploring multiple perspectives can be misinterpreted and lead to defensiveness or misunderstanding. It may be difficult to use newly developed critical thinking skills with other people who do not have those skills. Anticipating possible misunderstanding is helpful in developing prevention strategies in communication.

The following are some examples of types of responses in diversity-related discussions in the United States that can be problematic.

- People often see issues as having only two answers—one right and one wrong.
- Because of the dichotomous approach to issues, it is often easier to see the limitations of other perspectives than either (a) the limitations of one's own perspective or (b) the benefits of another perspective.
- People often are defensive or puzzled when they are asked why they believe something.
- People often use words like "moral" to avoid defining perspectives.
- Raising an alternative viewpoint is often interpreted as agreement with the viewpoint.
- People often claim majority agreement with their own opinion.

ACTIVITY 9.10

1. Speculate about the reasons for the following common responses in diversity-related discussions.

   a. "Whose side are you on, anyway?"

   b. "Everyone knows it is the right thing to do."

   c. "Why are you asking me to explain my opinion?"

   d. "This is just what I believe."

ACTIVITY 9.10, CONTINUED

2. Develop some possible responses to the statements in the previous question.

3. Add other statements that you have heard (or used) that hinder critical thinking in diversity discussions.

4. Develop some possible responses to the statements you heard (or used).

HOW TO MAINTAIN AND CONTINUE DIVERSITY LEARNING

Diversity learning does not stop at the end of a seminar or a college term. It is an ongoing process—there are always going to be new personal situations, new issues and new current events that can be used to apply diversity awareness and understanding.

It is important to consciously think about how you will maintain your increased level of awareness and understanding. There are many reasons why it may be difficult to maintain your diversity learning. It is easy to fall into patterns of disinterest, particularly if there is dissonance in maintaining an interest in diversity in your day-to-day life. Diversity issues may fall "off of your radar screen." You may have some failures in practicing diversity skills.

Example: Failed Practice

A student reported that while at a shopping mall, she saw an African-American man walking near her. Mindful of diversity issues that were discussed in class, she smiled and said "hello." The man proceeded to follow her around the mall, making her uncomfortable. She concluded that saying hello to African Americans was not a good idea.

ACTIVITY 9.11

Use the preceding example to respond to the following.

1. In what ways does the previous example represent failed practice? Did the student sabatoge her effort?

2. What could the student do differently next time?

ACTIVITY 9.12

1. What are your personal next steps in diversity learning?

2. What factors will allow you to maintain the progress you have made and move forward?

3. What do you think will be your greatest challenges in maintaining and continuing your diversity learning?

Evaluating Diversity Strategies in Your College or University

One way to apply diversity awareness and understanding is to evaluate your own institutional or professional culture. Examining the college or university you currently attend is one example of that type of application. The following activities are examples that can be used and adapted for other institutional settings.

ACTIVITY 9.13

1. When you selected your college or university, how important to you was the commitment of the college or university to diversity in your selection?

2. Describe your perceptions about your college or university in the following areas:

   a. commitment to diversity

   b. strategies for diversity

ACTIVITY 9.14

1. Examine the Internet web site of your university. Assume you are looking at the web site as a prospective student. For the following students, evaluate how the institutional culture would appear, using the questions below.

  a. a gay student

  b. a Jewish student

  c. a first-generation college student working to pay for school

  d. a 35-year-old student

  e. a person who uses a wheelchair

  f. an African-American student

  g. an Asian-American student

  h. you

ACTIVITY 9.14, CONTINUED

Note: For questions two through nine, select one person from question one. Specify which person you chose, and answer the questions (to the best of your ability) form the perspective of that person.

2. Do I see myself in the culture?

3. How do I see myself in the culture?

4. In what ways does the culture render me invisible?

5. Does the culture seem comfortable to me?

6. Would I be happy in this culture?

7. In what ways would I fit into this culture?

8. In what ways would I not fit into this culture?

9. Would I consider attending this university? Why or why not?

Activity 9.15

1. What activities are you involved in at the college or university (e.g., sports, sorority or fraternity)?

2. For each activity, what kinds of people do you think are most included and welcomed?

3. For each activity, what kinds of people do you think are not included and unwelcome?

4. For each activity, give examples of how the culture of the institution is supportive or not supportive.

"Silence Is Acceptance" Campaign

"Silence is acceptance" is the slogan for the efforts of one university to generate awareness and understanding of diversity issues. The slogan is used on buttons and posters across campus. Examining the meaning and implications of such a campaign is a good way to connect the personal choices of individuals with policy and institutional strategies.

Activity 9.16

1. What does "silence is acceptance" mean to you personally (e.g., silence about what, silence by whom, and what is acceptance)?

2. When (if ever) is silence not necessarily acceptance?

3. What are deterrents to speaking out (e.g., fear of ridicule, wanting to fit in, fear of physical danger)?

4. What behaviors should and should not be tolerated by the institution? Who/what is the institution?

5. What concepts intersect with "silence is acceptance" (e.g., free speech, freedom of expression, power differentials)?

Exploring the Meaning of a University Diversity Statement

Many colleges and universities have statements or policies on diversity. (An absence of such policies is a statement, too.) An in-depth exploration of diversity statements is a useful way to examine the varied meanings of policies from person to person.

ACTIVITY 9.17

1. In your opinion, what should university policies related to diversity include?

2. Select and read a document from your university. If there is not an explicit diversity statement, select a mission statement, a presidential address or a vision statement.

3. Are there parts of the document you think should be omitted?

4. What is not in the document that you think should be included?

5. Speculate about the meaning of the omissions you listed in the previous question. What values are reflected in the omissions?

6. In your opinion, why does the institution have the document?

7. What types of diversity are included in the document?

ACTIVITY **9.17**, CONTINUED

8. What types of diversity are not included in the document?

9. Identify words in the document that have varied cultural meanings (e.g., respect, tolerance).

10. What are the inherent values suggested in the document?

11. In what ways do the values suggested in the document represent your values?

12. In what ways do the values suggested in the document not represent your values?

13. In what ways are the goals and values expressed in the document explicitly carried out in the college or university?

14. In what ways are the goals and values expressed in the document not carried out in the college or university?

Putting It All Together

This chapter has focused on two key points. First, the chapter explored how to develop your own strategies for diversity awareness, understanding and application that are based on your personality, values and beliefs. Second, the chapter applied critical-thinking skills to the context of your college or university culture as a way to practice how those skills can be used in multiple situations and cultures. The following activities are designed to be completed near the end of the term.

ACTIVITY **9.18**

Use the following quote to respond to the following.

"There are two ways of spreading light: to be the candle or the mirror that reflects it."
(Edith Wharton)

1. What does the quote mean to you?

2. In what types of situations are you most comfortable being the candle?

3. In what types of situations are you most comfortable being the mirror?

4. What is a specific example of where you have been (or could be) the candle?

5. What is a specific example of where you have been (or could be) the mirror?

ACTIVITY 9.19

Read the Sojourner Truth quote at the beginning of the chapter. In the following questions, describe issues and strategies. Consider your own personality, time, resources, values and beliefs.

1. In what ways can you be "a flea for justice" with your friends and family?

2. In what ways can you be "a flea for justice" at your university?

3. In what ways can you be "a flea for justice" in your community?

4. In what ways can you be "a flea for justice" in your professional career?

ACTIVITY 9.20

(Source: Dr. Joan Fopma-Loy, Miami University)

1. Write a letter to yourself. In the letter, talk about what you want to remind yourself from the course. Put the letter in an envelope, seal and address the envelope to yourself. Give the envelope to your instructor, who will send you the letter in two months.

2. Use two colors of paper for this activity. On one color, write the legacy you would like to give future students in this class. The legacies from you and the other students in your section will be shared with the new students the first day of class next term. On the other color, write down what you feel are the most important things you have learned in the class.

(Note to instructor: See Instructor's Guide.)